# HMH SCIENCE DIMENSIONS™
## Volume 2

## Grade 4
## Units 6–8

This Write-In Book belongs to

_____

Teacher/Room

_____

W0010493

# Houghton Mifflin Harcourt™

# Consulting Authors

**Michael A. DiSpezio**
*Global Educator*
North Falmouth, Massachusetts

**Marjorie Frank**
*Science Writer and Content-Area
  Reading Specialist*
Brooklyn, New York

**Michael R. Heithaus, PhD**
*Dean, College of Arts, Sciences &
  Education*
*Professor, Department of Biological
  Sciences*
Florida International University
Miami, Florida

**Cary Sneider, PhD**
*Associate Research Professor*
Portland State University
Portland, Oregon

Front cover: model car ©GIPhotoStock/Science Source

Back cover: Mars Rover ©NASA/JPL/Cornell University/Maas Digital

Printed in the U.S.A.

ISBN  978-1-328-90456-0

11  0928  25 24 23 22

4500842425          C D E F G

## Program Advisors

**Paul D. Asimow, PhD**
*Eleanor and John R. McMillan*
*Professor of Geology and*
*Geochemistry*
California Institute of
Technology
Pasadena, California

**Eileen Cashman, PhD**
*Professor*
Humboldt State University
Arcata, California

**Mark B. Moldwin, PhD**
*Professor of Space Sciences and*
*Engineering*
University of Michigan
Ann Arbor, Michigan

**Kelly Y. Neiles, PhD**
*Assistant Professor of Chemistry*
St. Mary's College of Maryland
St. Mary's City, Maryland

**Sten Odenwald, PhD**
*Astronomer*
NASA Goddard Spaceflight
Center
Greenbelt, Maryland

**Bruce W. Schafer**
*Director of K–12 STEM*
*Collaborations, retired*
Oregon University System
Portland, Oregon

**Barry A. Van Deman**
*President and CEO*
Museum of Life and Science
Durham, North Carolina

**Kim Withers, PhD**
*Assistant Professor*
Texas A&M University-Corpus
Christi
Corpus Christi, Texas

**Adam D. Woods, PhD**
*Professor*
California State University,
Fullerton
Fullerton, California

## Classroom Reviewers

**Michelle Barnett**
Lichen K–8 School
Citrus Heights, California

**Brandi Bazarnik**
Skycrest Elementary
Citrus Heights, California

**Kristin Wojes-Broetzmann**
Saint Anthony Parish School
Menomonee Falls, Wisconsin

**Andrea Brown**
*District Science and STEAM*
*Curriculum TOSA*
Hacienda La Puente Unified
School District
Hacienda Heights, California

**Denice Gayner**
Earl LeGette Elementary
Fair Oaks, California

**Emily Giles**
*Elementary Curriculum*
*Consultant*
Kenton County School District
Ft. Wright, Kentucky

**Crystal Hintzman**
*Director of Curriculum,*
*Instruction and Assessment*
School District of Superior
Superior, Wisconsin

**Roya Hosseini**
Junction Avenue K–8 School
Livermore, California

**Cynthia Alexander Kirk**
*Classroom Teacher, Learning*
*Specialist*
West Creek Academy
Valencia, California

**Marie LaCross**
Fair Oaks Ranch Community
School
Santa Clarita, California

**Emily Miller**
*Science Specialist*
Madison Metropolitan School
District
Madison, Wisconsin

**Monica Murray, EdD**
*Principal*
Bassett Unified School District
La Puente, California

**Wendy Savaske**
*Director of Instructional*
*Services*
School District of Holmen
Holmen, Wisconsin

**Tina Topoleski**
*District Science Supervisor*
Jackson School District
Jackson, New Jersey

# You are a scientist!

## You are naturally curious.

*Have you wondered . . .*

• is ice still water?

• if you could float in midair?

• how you can talk to your friend on a cell phone?

• if plants can grow without soil?

_____

_____

_____

Write in some other things you wonder about.

# HMH SCIENCE DIMENSIONS™

## will SPARK your curiosity

### AND prepare you for

✓ tomorrow
✓ next year
✓ college or career
✓ life

## Where do you see yourself in 20 years?

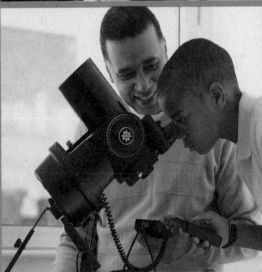

Write in or draw another career you'd like.

# Be a scientist.

## Work like real scientists work.

Plan

Investigate

Have Fun

# Be an engineer.

**Solve problems like engineers do.**

Design

Solve Problems

Share Solutions

# Explain your world.

Start by asking questions.

Think Critically

Make a Claim

Gather Evidence

# There's more than one way to the answer. What's YOURS?

Work in Teams

Develop Explanations

Support Your Conclusions

# Engineering and Technology .............................. 1

# Energy ......................................................... 65

© Houghton Mifflin Harcourt ○ Image Credits: ©NASA

# Changes to Earth's Surface ...349

# Rocks and Fossils ........................453

# Safety in the Lab

Doing science is a lot of fun. But, a science lab can be a dangerous place. Falls, cuts, and burns can happen easily. **Know the safety rules and listen to your teacher.**

☐ **Think ahead.** Study the investigation steps so you know what to expect. If you have any questions, ask your teacher. Be sure you understand all caution statements and safety reminders.

☐ **Be neat and clean.** Keep your work area clean. If you have long hair, pull it back so it doesn't get in the way. Roll or push up long sleeves to keep them away from your activity.

☐ **Oops!** If you spill or break something, or get cut, tell your teacher right away.

☐ **Watch your eyes.** Wear safety goggles anytime you are directed to do so. If you get anything in your eyes, tell your teacher right away.

☐ **Yuck!** Never eat or drink anything during a science activity.

☐ **Don't get shocked.** Be careful if an electric appliance is used. Be sure that electric cords are in a safe place where you can't trip over them. Never use the cord to pull a plug from an outlet.

☐ **Keep it clean.** Always clean up when you have finished. Put everything away and wipe your work area. Wash your hands.

☐ **Play it safe.** Always know where to find safety equipment, such as fire extinguishers. Know how to use the safety equipment around you.

# Safety in the Field

Lots of science research happens outdoors. It's fun to explore the wild! But, you need to be careful. The weather, the land, and the living things can surprise you.

☐ **Think ahead.** Study the investigation steps so you know what to expect. If you have any questions, ask your teacher. Be sure you understand all caution statements and safety reminders.

☐ **Dress right.** Wear appropriate clothes and shoes for the outdoors. Cover up and wear sunscreen and sunglasses for sun safety.

☐ **Clean up the area.** Follow your teacher's instructions for when and how to throw away waste.

☐ **Oops!** Tell your teacher right away if you break something or get hurt.

☐ **Watch your eyes.** Wear safety goggles when directed to do so. If you get anything in your eyes, tell your teacher right away.

☐ **Yuck!** Never taste anything outdoors.

☐ **Stay with your group.** Work in the area as directed by your teacher. Stay on marked trails.

☐ **"Wilderness" doesn't mean go wild.** Never engage in horseplay, games, or pranks.

☐ **Always walk.** No running!

☐ **Play it safe.** Know where safety equipment can be found and how to use it. Know how to get help.

☐ **Clean up.** Wash your hands with soap and water when you come back indoors.

# Safety Symbols

To highlight important safety concerns, the following symbols are used in a Hands-On Activity. Remember that no matter what safety symbols you see, all safety rules should be followed at all times.

## Dress Code

- Wear safety goggles as directed.
- If anything gets into your eye, tell your teacher immediately
- Do not wear contact lenses in the lab.
- Wear appropriate protective gloves as directed.
- Tie back long hair, secure loose clothing, and remove loose jewelry.

## Glassware and Sharp Object Safety

- Do not use chipped or cracked glassware.
- Notify your teacher immediately if a piece of glass breaks.
- Use extreme care when handling all sharp and pointed instruments.
- Do not cut an object while holding the object in your hands.
- Cut objects on a suitable surface, always in a direction away from your body.

## Electrical Safety

- Do not use equipment with frayed electrical cords or loose plugs.
- Do not use electrical equipment near water or when clothing or hands are wet.
- Hold the plug when you plug in or unplug equipment.

## Chemical Safety

- If a chemical gets on your skin, on your clothing, or in your eyes, rinse it immediately, and tell your teacher.
- Do not clean up spilled chemicals unless your teacher directs you to do so.
- Keep your hands away from your face while you are working on any activity.

## Heating and Fire Safety

- Know your school's evacuation-fire routes.
- Never leave a hot plate unattended while it is turned on or while it is cooling.
- Allow equipment to cool before storing it.

## Plant and Animal Safety

- Do not eat any part of a plant.
- Do not pick any wild plant unless your teacher instructs you to do so.
- Treat animals carefully and respectfully.
- Wash your hands throughly after handling any plant or animal.

## Cleanup

- Clean all work surfaces and protective equipment as directed by your teacher.
- Wash your hands throughly before you leave the lab or after any activity.

# Safety Quiz

**Circle the letter of the BEST answer.**

1. Before starting an activity, you should
   a. try an experiment of your own.
   b. open all containers and packages.
   c. read all directions and make sure you understand them.
   d. handle all the equipment to become familiar with it.

2. At the end of any activity you should
   a. wash your hands thoroughly before leaving the lab.
   b. cover your face with your hands.
   c. put on your safety goggles.
   d. leave the materials where they are.

3. If you get hurt or injured in any way, you should
   a. tell your teacher immediately.
   b. find bandages or a first aid kit.
   c. go to your principal's office.
   d. get help after you finish the activity.

4. If your equipment is chipped or broken, you should
   a. use it only for solid materials.
   b. give it to your teacher for recycling or disposal.
   c. put it back.
   d. increase the damage so that it is obvious.

5. If you have unused liquids after finishing an activity, you should
   a. pour them down a sink or drain.
   b. mix them all together in a bucket.
   c. put them back into their original containers.
   d. dispose of them as directed by your teacher.

6. When working with materials that might fly into the air and hurt someone's eye, you should wear
   a. goggles.
   b. an apron.
   c. gloves.
   d. a hat.

7. If you get something in your eye you should
   a. wash your hands immediately.
   b. put the lid back on the container.
   c. wait to see if your eye becomes irritated.
   d. tell your teacher right away.

# Changes to Earth's Surface

**Explore Online**

**Unit Project: Nearby Weathering**
What are some examples of weathering right near your school, and how can you affect them? You will conduct an investigation with your team. Ask your teacher for details.

The surface of our Earth changes constantly, in countless ways. Much of that change is gradual. Some of it, such as

# At a Glance

## Vocabulary Game: Guess the Word

**Materials**
- kitchen timer or online computer timer

**Directions**

1. Take turns by choosing a word card. Do not tell others the word. Set the timer for one minute.

2. Point to another player. Give them a one-word clue to use to guess the word.

3. Repeat step 2 until the word is guessed or time runs out. Give a different clue each time.

4. One point is earned for guessing the word and 1 more point if they use the word in a sentence. That player gets the next turn choosing a word.

5. The first player to score 5 points wins.

**desert**

An area of land that is very dry.

**ocean trench**

A deep valley in the ocean floor.

# Unit Vocabulary

 **continent:** One of the seven largest land areas on Earth.

 **ocean trench:** A deep valley in the ocean floor.

 **deposition:** The dropping or settling of eroded materials.

 **rain forest:** A dense forest found in regions with high heat and heavy rainfall.

 **desert:** An area of land that is very dry.

 **scale:** The part of a map that compares a distance on the map to a distance in the real world.

 **elevation:** The height of the land above sea level.

 **weathering:** The breaking down of rocks on Earth's surface into smaller pieces.

 **erosion:** The process of moving sediment from one place to another.

# How Does Water Shape Earth's Surface?

People from around the world come to visit the Grand Canyon. Look at the photo above. What are some features of the landscape that you notice?

_____

**By the end of this lesson . . .**
you'll be able to explain how Earth processes shape the land.

## Can You Explain It?

A river flows through the bottom of this canyon. Think about how the canyon
may have formed. Imagine walking through the bottom of the canyon, near the
river. What would you see and hear?

**1.** How do you think this canyon formed? What could have reshaped the rock ?

_____

_____

_____

_____

_____

_____

_____

 **EVIDENCE NOTEBOOK** Look for this icon to help you gather evidence
to answer the questions above.

# Making a Move

## Watery Trails

A river is a stream of water that flows within a channel. A river starts at its source and ends at its mouth. In between these points, the width, volume, and flow of the river changes. These changes happen over time.

Hills and mountains are the source for many rivers. The riverbed has a steep slope, and its valley is narrow. As a result, the river flows downhill fast. The flowing river picks up small rocks and soil known as *sediment*. Other rivers may join the original river, making it wider. As a river nears its mouth, it slows down and drops sediment. A large area of flat land known as a *delta* may form here.

▷ **Explore Online**

**Step 1:** The images on these pages show one way that a river can change through various processes.

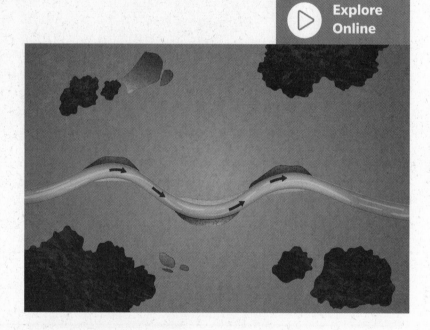

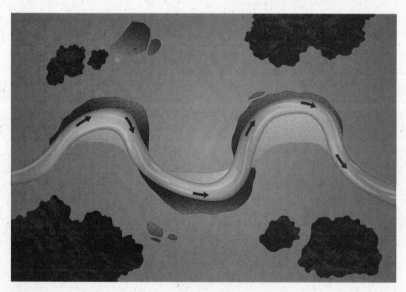

**Step 2:** As it flows downstream, the river is forming curves and bends as sediment is picked up in one place and dropped in another. The dark areas show where sediment is being picked up. The lighter areas are where it is being dropped. These processes are changing the course of the river.

© Houghton Mifflin Harcourt

**Step 3:** Moving water continues to shape the river. It has nearly formed a loop. Look back at how the river began. Notice how much these processes have changed the river!

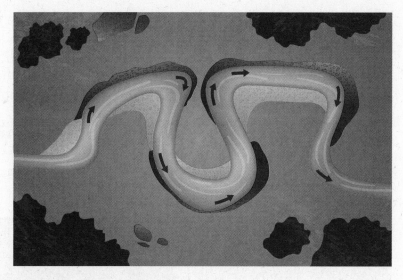

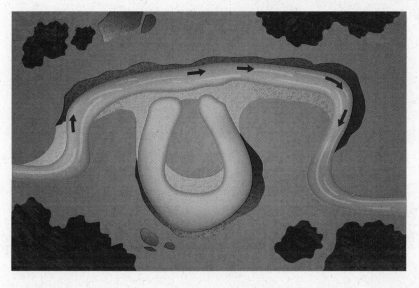

**Step 4:** Over time, this river has changed its course. Part of the old course has been cut off. The water left in the old path forms a lake known as an oxbow lake. Over time, it may dry up.

**2.** Choose the best word or phrase to complete each sentence.

| steep | flat | wider | narrower | banks |
|-------|------|-------|----------|-------|
| mouths | curves | meander | floodplain | deltas |

The slope of a river is often _____ near its source. The river gets

_____ as other rivers and streams enter it. Rivers sometimes form

_____ as they flow through these flat areas. Rivers slow down near

their mouths, dropping sediment to form _____ .

 **EVIDENCE NOTEBOOK** You've learned about some changes caused by rivers. In your Evidence Notebook, explain how this information might relate to the canyon you saw at the beginning of the lesson.

# Over Its Banks

What happens to rain once it hits the ground? Some sinks in. Some runs into rivers, lakes, and the ocean. If rain is heavy, a river can flow over its banks. This causes flooding. Flooding can cause many things to happen.

## Effects of a Flood

**3.** Read the descriptions and look at the picture. Then label the part of the picture that matches each description.

**a.** The flood has killed crops in this field, but the floodwaters also drop sediment that contains nutrients. This makes rich soil that is good for future crops.

**b.** Most of the time, this river flows between its banks where the trees are. When water flows over the banks, flooding occurs.

**c.** Floodwaters can cover roads and damage houses, schools, and other buildings. Water may enter basements and the first floor of some buildings.

**d.** In a flash flood, more water than normal rushes down a river. The rushing water is strong enough to damage low bridges over the river.

# Water Effects

4. Research to find images of ways that floods can damage roads. What do you notice about the roads and what they are made of? Do you think that floodwaters could break other things into pieces? Use evidence from your research to support your response.

Water has damaged this road.

## Putting it Together

Select all the answers that apply for each question.

5. Why does the flow of a river slow down near its mouth?
   a. It flows over flat land.
   b. It is full of stones and gravel.
   c. It is entering a larger body of water.
   d. It is flowing through a steep channel.

6. When do bends form in a river?
   a. when the river first forms
   b. when the river flows very fast
   c. when the river is getting older
   d. when the river flows over a broad, flat area

7. What effects can flooding have?
   a. Streets are covered with water.
   b. Floodwater enters houses.
   c. Rainfall is heavier than normal.
   d. Soil washes away.

8. What are positive effects of flooding?
   a. Floodwaters drop sediment that is rich in nutrients.
   b. Curves form in a river.
   c. Water flows very slowly down a river.
   d. Good farmland forms on floodplains.

# Away It Goes!

## Vanishing Cottages

These pictures show a seaside town in England named Birling Gap. The town is near cliffs by the sea. The cliffs are made of a very soft rock called chalk. Strong waves pound the cliffs, especially during storms.

**1905:** This picture shows several houses at Birling Gap. They are a short distance from a cliff that drops into the sea.

**1930s:** Compare this photo to the photo from 1905. You can see that some of the cliff has fallen away.

**1970s:** In this photo from the 1970s, more of the cliff has disappeared.

**2015:** Look at how the distance of the houses from the edge of the cliff has changed.

 **9. Language SmArts** Use the images above to help you answer these questions. What happened to the distance between the houses and the cliff between 1905 and 2015? What do you think caused this change?

_____

_____

_____

# Watch It Go!

Several processes constantly change Earth's surface. Three of these processes are described below.

- **Weathering** is the breaking down of rocks on Earth's surface into smaller pieces. Weathering occurs in rivers when the current causes rocks to bump against each other and break apart. Weathering can also occur in other ways.

- **Erosion** is the process of moving weathered rock and soil from one place to another. This happens when rivers move rock and soil downstream. Factors such as wind and gravity can also cause erosion.

- **Deposition** occurs when water slows down and drops the rocks and sediment it carries. This occurs at the mouth of rivers and anywhere water stops moving.

**10.** In the images below, circle where the change is taking place.

**11.** Choose the word or phrase to complete each sentence.

> erosion    weathering    deposition

When rock from a cliff cracks,

_____ occurs. When the

rock falls, _____ occurs.

Finally, the rock settles on the land

below. This is called _____.

# Water Power

As you've seen, water helps shape the land through weathering, erosion, and deposition. Rivers change the areas they flow through. Flooding can move sediment. Waves can crumble cliffs.

There are many factors that can affect the rates of weathering, erosion, and deposition. The amount of water, the angle of a slope, and rate of the deposition can all affect how quickly these processes occur.

## Changing the Shape of Land

**12.** Look at the images below, and label them with letters for the correct descriptions shown at the top of the next page.

Explore Online

**a.** Heavy rain can cause **mudslides,** or the quick movement of rain-soaked soil downhill. Mudslides are a type of erosion. When the ground is steep, water and mud can slide down faster. As a result, there is more erosion.

**b.** **Waves** cause both weathering and erosion on rocky beaches. The force of the pounding waves splits and chips rock. Then the water carries the pieces away.

**c.** A **swiftly flowing stream** causes erosion. The moving water carries sediment and rocks downstream.

**d.** **Falling water** weathers the stone under the falls. Erosion causes pieces of rock to drop away. Then deposition piles the rocks up under the falling water. When weathering happens quickly, erosion and deposition happen quickly, too.

 **EVIDENCE NOTEBOOK** You've learned about ways that water can cause weathering and erosion. In your Evidence Notebook, make a list that summarizes this information. Then write a sentence or two for each entry on your list, explaining how it provides evidence for how a canyon is formed.

 **Language SmArts**
# Categorizing Information

**Tip**

The English Language Arts Handbook can provide help with understanding how to categorize information.

**13.** Complete the table with these possible causes and effects: *waves, swift current, mudslide,* or *flooding.*

| Cause | Effect |
|---|---|
| | Sediment is deposited on farmland. |
| Heavy rain pours down a steep slope of bare soil. | |
| | Weathering splits and breaks the rock of a cliff. |
| | Erosion occurs as rocks move downstream. |

# Cold Stuff!

## Water, Ice, and Water

Explore Online

Liquid water becomes ice when its temperature drops to 0 °C or below. When its temperature rises above 0 °C, the ice thaws and becomes liquid water again. In nature, this cycle of freezing and thawing happens constantly. Can this pattern of freezing and thawing cause weathering and erosion? Look at the images on this and the next page to find out!

1 There are small cracks in the surface of this rock.

2 Precipitation fills cracks in the rock with water. This usually happens after rain falls or snow melts.

3 If the temperature falls below 0 °C, water in the cracks freezes. The liquid water becomes solid ice. What happens when the ice presses against the sides of the crack?

**4**

**5**

When the temperature rises above 0 °C, the ice melts. Compare the crack now to the original crack.

The crack is now wider than before. After this pattern repeats many times, pieces may break off and be carried away.

**HANDS-ON** Apply What You Know

# Watching Water Grow

14. Fill a clear plastic cup halfway with water. Use a permanent marker to make a line on the side of the cup where the top of the water is. Place the cup in the freezer overnight. The following day, take the cup out of the freezer. Observe the top of the water. Is it the same place where you drew the line? If not, can you explain why?

Language SmArts
# Recalling Information

15. Predict what will happen to the rock as the pattern of freezing and thawing continues. Use information from these pages or personal experience to support your prediction.

_____

_____

_____

_____

_____

# Pushing Through

A glacier is a river of ice moving downhill very slowly. Glaciers are found in the coldest parts of Earth—the cold polar zones or cold, high mountain valleys.

Glaciers look like they are standing still. But they are slowly moving—so slowly that you can't see the movement with your eyes alone. But as glaciers move, they can change the land—just like running water. Glaciers weather rock beneath them. They scrape and cut rock they slide over. They cause erosion by pushing the broken pieces of rock under them and on top of them as they move. Deposition occurs when glaciers melt and leave the rock they carried behind.

As this glacier moves, it pushes rocks along with it.

Glaciers change the land they flow through.

As the ice melts, glaciers also leave sediment behind.

16. The freezing and melting of water causes changes. The movement of glaciers does, too. Compare and contrast the two processes.

|  | Glacier | Freezing and thawing |
|---|---|---|
| **Speed** |  |  |
| **Effect** |  |  |
| **Area covered** |  |  |

17. Use the evidence in your completed table to explain which process has a greater effect on the land.

_____

_____

_____

_____

 **EVIDENCE NOTEBOOK** Think about what you've learned about how glaciers shape the land. Consider the canyon you saw at the beginning of the lesson. In your Evidence Notebook, explain whether or not the canyon could have been formed by glaciers. Support your explanation with evidence.

## Putting It Together

18. The statements below describe some of the causes and effects of ice. Draw a line to match the causes in the left column to the correct effect in the right column.

- Glaciers move downhill.

- Glaciers scrape over rocks under them.

- Water freezes inside cracks in rock.

- Glacier ice melts.

- Erosion occurs as broken rocks are moved elsewhere.

- Weathering occurs as rocks crack and break.

- Deposition occurs as sediment is left behind.

- Weathering occurs as the water freezes and expands, making cracks bigger.

# The Rate of Change

## Objective

**Collaborate** with a partner to investigate the effect of slope on erosion.

What question will you investigate to meet this objective?

_____

_____

_____

© Houghton Mifflin Harcourt

### Materials
- paper cup
- sharpened pencil
- plastic drinking straw
- scissors
- small piece of modeling clay
- piece of cardboard 31 cm square
- soil
- ruler
- large bottle filled with water (approx. 2 liters)

## Procedure

**STEP 1** Working with a partner, carefully punch a hole near the bottom of the cup with the pencil. Use the scissors to cut a couple of inches from the straw. Push the straw into the hole. Press the clay around the straw to seal any openings around it.

Why is it important to seal the hole with clay?

_____

_____

_____

**STEP 2** Place the piece of cardboard on the ground. Mound some dirt under one end of the cardboard to raise it about 2 inches off the ground so that the cardboard has a slight slope.

How would you describe the slope of the cardboard?

_____

_____

_____

**STEP 3** Spread a thin layer of soil over the cardboard. Place the cup on the raised end of the cardboard, with the straw pointing downslope. Block the end of the straw with your finger, while your partner fills the cup with water.

What does the water in the cup model?

_____

_____

_____

**STEP 4** Take your finger off the straw, and allow the water to flow out. Observe how fast the water flows and the shape of the stream. Record your results in the box below.

How does the flow of the water affect the soil on the cardboard?

_____

_____

_____

_____

| Observations: Step 4 | |
|---|---|
| | |

**STEP 5** Now raise the high end of the cardboard to about 6 inches so that it has a steeper slope than before. Repeat step 4 for this second trial. Record your results on the next page.

What does this set of steps model?

_____

_____

_____

_____

| Observations: Step 5 | |
|---|---|
| | |

## Analyze Your Results

**STEP 6**  Did water flow over a steeper slope or a lower slope produce more erosion?

_____

_____

**STEP 7**  Compare your results to the results of other groups. Describe any similarities or differences you notice.

_____

_____

**STEP 8**  State a claim that is related to your question at the beginning of this activity.

_____

_____

## Draw Conclusions

**STEP 9**  Cite evidence to support your claim.

_____

_____

**STEP 10**  What other questions do you have about the ways in which scientists study erosion?

_____

_____

# What about Us?

## At the Beach

Look at the photos below. They show waves hitting a beach. Recall what you have learned about weathering, erosion, and deposition. Do you see any of these processes in the photos?

▷ Explore Online

Waves in the ocean roll onto the shore. The waves move sand over the beach. They also bring with them bits and pieces of rocks and shells and leave them on the shore. Then the tide pulls the water back. Some of the material it deposited is washed back into the ocean. Erosion and deposition change the shape and slope of beaches.

### Beach Weathering

19. Choose the word that correctly completes each sentence in the paragraph.

| erosion | deposition | weathering |

Beach sand forms from the _____, or breaking down, of rock.

Waves move sand along the beach, causing _____.

In some places, sand washes from the beach into the ocean. In other places,

_____ leaves new sand on the beach.

# On the Road

**20.** Look at the parts of two roads below. One road is in a place with a cold winter climate. The other road is in a place where the winter climate is warmer. Label the region each pair of images comes from.

_____

No matter how smooth pavement is, small cracks cover the surface of the road.

When precipitation falls, the small cracks fill with different forms of water: liquid or ice.

_____

Small cracks cover the surface of the road.

When it rains, cracks in the road fill with water.

 **EVIDENCE NOTEBOOK** Study the surface of a sidewalk or road. Describe its surface in your Evidence Notebook. Explain how any cracks you observe may have occurred.

If the temperature drops below freezing, the water freezes and the cracks expand.

When temperatures rise and the ice melts, the cracks are wider than before.

The temperature stays above freezing, so the water remains liquid.

The road is dry, and the cracks are the same size as before the rain.

**21.** Explain the reasoning you used to label the roads.

_____

_____

_____

_____

### Engineer It!
# Fighting Potholes

Potholes are holes that form in roads due to weathering and erosion. One way that civil engineers might be able to stop potholes is by building smart roads. These roads are built with sensors in them. The sensors send information about traffic and road damage. When the information is received, needed repairs can take place before potholes get too big.

Reader

Self Powered Sensor Array

**22.** What other useful information could these sensors in the roads gather?

_____

_____

_____

## Putting It Together

**23.** Choose the best word or phrase to complete the paragraph.

| weathering | erosion | deposition |
|---|---|---|

When waves move sand over beaches, _____

occurs. Beaches also show _____ when waves

leave behind sand and bits of other material they carry. These

processes change the shape and slope of beaches.

**24.** Choose the best word or phrase to complete the paragraph.

| thaws | flows | freezes |
|---|---|---|
| closes | expands | melts |
| hot | mild | cold |

Changing temperatures can affect the condition of roads. Water

_____ and thaws inside cracks in roads. Ice

_____ in the cracks, just as it does in rock. As a result,

roads in _____ climates often show winter damage.

# Discover More

**Check out this path . . . or go online to choose one of these other paths.**

**People in Science & Engineering**

- Deposition Rate
- The Last Ice Age

## Anjali Fernandes

Dr. Anjali Fernandes researches to learn how Earth's surface changes over different time periods. She studies how sediment is transported and where it is deposited in both land and water environments.

Dr. Fernandes specializes in the formation and changes of channels. A channel is a landform caused by water cutting into Earth. Channels can form over long periods of time by slow-moving water, or quickly by fast-moving floods.

One method Dr. Fernandes uses in her studies is field research. This means she goes to where channels exist and studies them. She also uses laboratory experiments to learn about the movement of sediments and how sediments are deposited in channels.

**Explore Online**

Dr . Anjali Fernandes studies Earth's changing surface.

**25.** Think of a question you would like to ask Dr. Fernandes about her work.

_____

_____

_____

_____

**26.** Dr. Fernandes does both field work and laboratory experiments. If you were a scientist, do you think you would enjoy field work or laboratory work more? Why?

_____

_____

_____

**27.** What kinds of changes in Earth's surface would you most like to study?

_____

_____

_____

## Do the Math
## Measuring Erosion

Each year, water erodes the cliff beneath Horseshoe Falls, Canada. Horseshoe Falls is part of the larger Niagara Falls. Between the years 1842 and 1905, erosion was constant at about 1.16 meters (3.8 feet) per year.

**28.** During the 63 years between 1842 and 1905, how much did Horsehoe Falls erode in meters? In feet?

# Lesson Check

Name _____

## Can You Explain It?

**Explore Online**

1. Now that you've learned about how water shapes Earth's surface, explain how you think the canyon formed. Be sure to do the following:

   • Explain how the river is involved in the formation of the canyon.

   • Describe the role of weathering and erosion in the formation of the canyon.

   • Describe how weathering and erosion have changed the canyon over time.

 **EVIDENCE NOTEBOOK** Use the information you've collected in your Evidence Notebook to help cover each point above.

_____
_____
_____
_____
_____
_____
_____

## Checkpoints

Answer the questions about how weathering, erosion, and deposition change Earth's surface. Choose the best answers to the questions.

2. Which of these would speed up erosion?
   a. warmer temperatures
   b. steeper river channels
   c. a river with a fast current
   d. deposition of sediment

**Choose the best answer to each question.**

3. How do floods affect the environment? Select all that apply.
   a. Floods destroy buildings.
   b. Floods create areas of more fertile soil.
   c. Floods speed up the weathering of rock.
   d. Floods make riverbeds steeper.

4. Where does a river develop curves?
   a. in places where there are big rocks
   b. in places where it has the steepest slope
   c. where sediment is dropped at its mouth
   d. in the flat, wide areas of its course

5. Write the word in each blank that makes the sentences correct.

   | erosion | weathering | deposition |
   |---|---|---|

   When a river moves rock downstream, the process is called _____.

   Glaciers can grind over rock and break them in a process called _____.

   In the process of _____, water or ice drops rock or sediment that it has

   carried, causing landforms, such as deltas, to form.

6. Write the word in each blank that makes the sentences correct.

   | contracts | expands | |
   |---|---|---|
   | erosion | weathering | deposition |

   Water _____ when it freezes. As a result, _____

   occurs when ice forms inside the cracks in rock. The ice widens cracks and often

   breaks the rock.

# Lesson Roundup

**A.** Write the word or phrase in each blank that makes the sentences correct.

| mountains | valleys | slowly |
|---|---|---|
| quickly | break apart | join together |

Many rivers have their source in _____ . The riverbed has a steep

slope. As a result, the river flows downhill _____ and in a straight

path. As the river flows, it moves rocks and pebbles in the riverbed. The rocks

_____ as they smash into each other and move downstream.

. . . . . . . . . . . . . . . . . . . . . . . . . . . . . . . . . . . . . . . . . . . . . . . . . . . . . . . . . . . . . . . . . . . . . . . . . . . . . . . .

**B.** Describe one way that weathering, erosion, and deposition are similar.

_____

. . . . . . . . . . . . . . . . . . . . . . . . . . . . . . . . . . . . . . . . . . . . . . . . . . . . . . . . . . . . . . . . . . . . . . . . . . . . . . . .

**C.** Write the word or phrase in each blank that makes the sentences correct.

| mountains | slowly | weathering | |
|---|---|---|---|
| lakes | quickly | erosion | deposition |

Glaciers move _____ along the land. During their journey,

they break up rock beneath them, which is called _____. They

cause _____ as they move sand and rock along their path. In

addition, glaciers leave mounds of dirt and rock behind in a process called

_____.

. . . . . . . . . . . . . . . . . . . . . . . . . . . . . . . . . . . . . . . . . . . . . . . . . . . . . . . . . . . . . . . . . . . . . . . . . . . . . . . .

**D.** Which of the statements about beach sand are correct? Choose all that apply.
   **a.** It is formed by the weathering of rock.
   **b.** Waves erode it and deposit it in new places.
   **c.** It is mostly eroded by glaciers.
   **d.** It is formed by freezing and thawing.

# How Do Other Factors Shape Earth's Surface?

Rocks are very hard. You cannot mold them like clay, but they can change. Over long periods of time, weathering can break rock down into sand.

**By the end of this lesson . . .**
you'll identify, explain, and record evidence of weathering, erosion, and deposition.

## Can You Explain It?

 **Explore Online**

This rock is found in Bolivia. It is called Árbol de Piedra which means stone tree. The top of the rock is very large, but it sits firmly on a narrower column of rock.

**1.** How do you think natural processes on Earth's surface formed this rock? Why is it shaped this way?

_____

_____

_____

_____

_____

_____

_____

**Tip**

Learn more about Earth's features and how they are shaped in *How Does Water Shape Earth's Surface?*

 **EVIDENCE NOTEBOOK** Look for this icon to help you gather evidence to answer the questions above.

# Organisms and Environments

## Water World

The presence and movement of water can change Earth's surface in direct ways, such as the sea eroding a sandy beach or a river carving a canyon into the land. But water can also allow organisms to live, grow, and thrive, and those organisms can change Earth's surface.

Explore Online

**Deserts** get less than 26 centimeters (10 inches) of precipitation per year. Since living things need water to survive and grow, this limits the number of plants, animals, and other organisms that can live here.

**Rain forests** get 203 centimeters (80 inches) or more of rain in a year. This allows a tremendous number of different organisms to live here. Think about how a single tree in the rain forest could itself be an environment for other organisms.

2. What differences did you notice between the rain forest and the desert? Why do you think the amount of water is such an important factor in determining the number of organisms in these environments?

_____

_____

_____

_____

**Bactrian camels** live in the rocky deserts of Central and East Asia. When water is scarce, the camel can convert the stores of fat in its two humps to water and energy. This allows Bactrian camels to live without access to drinking water for months if necessary. When drinking water is found, they can drink 135 liters (30 gallons) in just half an hour! They will also eat snow and ice and just about any plant life they can find.

**The sambar deer** is a large animal that lives in parts of South and Southeast Asia. It lives in a variety of different forests, from tropical dry forests to tropical rain forests. Sambars prefer to be near water, where they can find many different plants to eat.

**3.** How do you think the adaptations of these animals help them survive in the environment in which they live?

_____

_____

_____

 **HANDS-ON  Apply What You Know**

## Dry Plants

**4.** The saguaro is a type of cactus that lives in the southwest. Despite the extreme temperatures and dry weather of the desert, the saguaro can grow up to 70 feet tall! Do some research to find two key features that help the saguaro thrive in its environment.

# Living Things Change Their Environments

Think about a ball field where kids play games, such as soccer or football. There may be patches of dirt where shoes have worn away the grass. Or perhaps you've walked on a trail through the woods and observed how it seems rockier and worn down after a rainstorm, while the surrounding area doesn't seem affected.

Animals, plants, and other organisms can have similar effects on the physical features of Earth's surface. Look at the images to see how organisms affect their environment.

This plant uses its roots to anchor itself in place and get water from the ground. As the roots grow, they can widen the cracks of the rock. Eventually, a chunk of rock may split off and fall.

Meerkats live in burrows. Digging a burrow creates a hole in the ground and moves dirt to the surface. This dirt may blow away, be carried by rainwater, or mixed with the dirt at the surface. It also exposes more rock that can then be weathered and eroded.

 **EVIDENCE NOTEBOOK** Consider what you've learned about plants and animals. Is there any evidence that either played a role in the formation of the "stone tree"?

Ivy is a type of plant that grows up and around other objects, including rock walls, fences, telephone poles, statues, homes, and trees. As ivy climbs, it sends out small roots that change their shape to cling to the surface the ivy is climbing. These roots can push into cracks in rock.

The root hairs give off a glue-like substance and feature hook-like structures on their tips. The root hairs can also dry up and twist into shapes that anchor the roots more firmly into the surface cracks.

Select which processes are described in each example. Circle all that apply.

**5.** an animal digging a burrow in the soil of a forest

   **a.** weathering          **b.** erosion          **c.** deposition

**6.** when a tree's roots grow in a crack of a boulder and the boulder breaks into two pieces

   **a.** weathering          **b.** erosion          **c.** deposition

 **7. Language SmArts** Conduct research to learn more about how ivy affects its environment. Write your findings below.

_____

_____

_____

# Other Ways Organisms Change Environments

You've looked at how organisms can be forces of erosion, weathering, and deposition. Now it's time to see other impacts organisms can have on their environments.

## Organism Cause and Effect

**8.** Look at the images to learn how some organisms change their environment. Then write the effects caused by these changes.

Beavers are dam builders. By toppling trees across streams, they cause the level of water behind the dam to rise.

_____

_____

_____

This type of termite builds large mounds out of soil. The termites live and reproduce in the mounds, which can be tall and narrow or a hundred feet wide. When the mound erodes due to wind or rain, the termites deposit fresh soil to replace what was lost.

_____

_____

_____

_____

Prairie grasses cover the landscape in the Great Plains. When a river floods its banks, the grasses' roots help keep the wet soil in place.

_____

_____

_____

 **Language SmArts**

# Understand Cause and Effect

**9.** Think about the photos and information in this section. Fill in the chart below with the missing cause or effect.

| Cause | Effect |
|---|---|
| The amount of water in an environment goes up. | |
| | Ivy roots can cause weathering when they grow into rock. |
| Beavers build dams. | |

© Houghton Mifflin Harcourt • Image Credits: (inset) ©Glenn Bartley/Getty Images; (t) ©HayleyMorton1/istock/getty Images Plus/Getty Images

**Tip**

The English Language Arts Handbook can provide help with understanding how cause and effect works.

# Environments Change

## Blast Off!

The photo shows a sandblaster in use. Think about what natural process may have inspired the invention of the first sandblaster.

**Engineer It!**

## Blast It Off

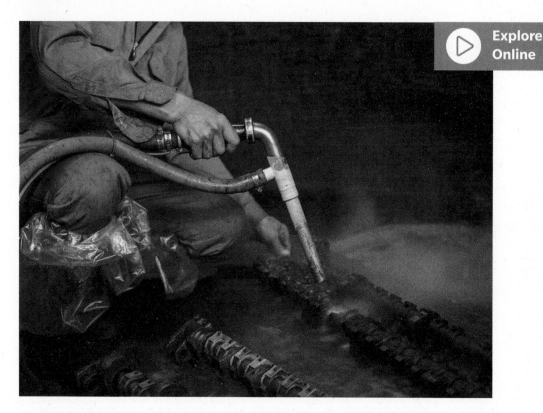

Explore Online

Sandblasting is a technique for removing paint, rust, or other coatings from things such as cars, steel beams, pipes, and other objects. Sandblasting can smooth a rough surface or roughen a smooth surface. Compressed air is used to spray sand at an object at high speed. The friction from the sand hitting the object physically blasts particles off the object's surface.

**10.** How do you think the sandblaster compares to weathering and erosion?

_____

_____

_____

## A Slower Process

**11.** With guidance from your teacher, use a piece of sandpaper to remove rust, paint, or some other substance from a piece of metal or wood. Keep track of how much time you spend actively sanding the material and how much debris ends up on the sandpaper or the table. Compare the results of your effort with what you saw in the sandblaster photo. Explain which factors might account for the differences between sandblasting and sanding by hand.

In places that receive very little precipitation, there isn't much erosion, weathering, or deposition that's caused by water or organisms. But rock and sediment in these places can still be eroded and weathered by other forces.

### Desert Erosion

**12.** Look at the image below. Circle the spots where you think weathering and erosion may occur.

Explore Online

# The Sands of Time

Look at the images that follow. They show the results of weathering, erosion, and deposition over time. These factors contribute to changes in Earth's surface.

## Changes Over Time

**13.** Choose the factor that is involved in each example.

**a.** Wind transports sand across the landscape. Some of the sand comes into contact with parts of a large boulder. Over time, the boulder becomes eroded.

    **a.** wind weathering the boulder

    **b.** windblown sand eroding the lower part of the boulder

    **c.** moving water eroding the lower part of the boulder

**b.** Wind can transport sand and other types of sediment from the base of a hill.

    **a.** wind erosion on the lower part of the slope

    **b.** deposition of sand at the top of the slope

    **c.** gravity pulling down on the rocks

**c.** As sand is transported across a landscape by wind, it can build up in certain areas.

    **a.** deposition of sand

    **b.** weathering of sand

    **c.** moving water deposits sand and erodes dunes

**14.** You know that deserts are dry environments. Make a claim about whether or not you think water ever changes a desert landscape.

_____

_____

_____

**a.** Cite one piece of evidence to support your claim.

_____

_____

_____

**b.** Cite another piece of evidence to support your claim.

_____

_____

_____

 **EVIDENCE NOTEBOOK** Think about the ways the desert landscape changed. What ideas do you have about how the tree rock you saw at the beginning of this lesson formed? Record your ideas in your notebook.

# Gravity and Weathering

Let's take a closer look at how wind and gravity can cause changes to the land.

## A Closer Look

**15.** Use the descriptions below to label the desert scene after the processes of weathering, erosion, and deposition have changed the landscape.

**a.** Sand dunes build up where windblown sand was deposited in certain spots. The dunes act as a wall that catches some of the sand that's being blown around.

**b.** Over time, sand blown around the desert environment eroded the lower part of the rock. Gravity prevented much of the sand from rising high enough in the air to hit the higher part of the rock.

**c.** Wind eroded the lower portion of the hillside. Once the lower portion was gone, the force of gravity pulled the upper portion down into the empty space.

 **16. Language SmArts** Use information to identify which of these formations were affected by gravity. How did gravity affect these processes?

_____

_____

© Houghton Mifflin Harcourt

17. Which of the following sentences best describes erosion caused by wind?
   a. Soot particles from a smokestack are carried through the air and deposited into the sea.
   b. Wind picks up particles of dry topsoil from a farm and carries them many miles away.
   c. A child shovels beach sand high into the air and watches it land on the sand dune.
   d. Arctic air moves in and freezes water in the cracks of a rock, causing the rock to break into small pieces.

18. Which of the following forms of erosion is caused by gravity?
   a. landslide after the lower hillside is eroded
   b. wind blowing against sandstone cliffs
   c. waves striking a sandy beach
   d. sand dune built up by sand deposition

## Putting it Together

19. Read each sentence. Circle true or false.

| | | | |
|---|---|---|---|
| a. Wind is a force that can build and move sand dunes. | True | False |
| b. If a large sand dune or other type of hill has part of the lower slope moved away, gravity will cause material higher on the slope to tumble down. | True | False |
| c. The sand tumbling down is called a sand dune. | True | False |
| d. When snow melts on a mountain, gravity pulls the meltwater downhill, which weathers sediment and carries it to a new place. | True | False |
| e. When the water reaches a relatively flat area, gravity causes the sediment to sink or settle in that new place. | True | False |
| f. Plants do not affect weathering. | True | False |
| g. Water in the process of carrying sediment is known as deposition. | True | False |
| h. Erosion can be caused by animal activity. | True | False |

## HANDS-ON ACTIVITY
# Finding Change

## Objective

**Collaborate** with your team to model processes that produce change on Earth's surface, and determine what kinds of evidence those processes leave behind.

What question will you investigate to meet this objective?

_____

_____

### Materials
- 4 cookie sheets with raised edge
- sand
- fan
- ice cubes
- modeling clay
- wooden stirring sticks
- beaker or small jug of water
- ruler

## Procedure

**STEP 1**  Go to the station your teacher assigns you to. Make observations of the model at your station. Record your observations. Then rotate through the other stations and record your initial observations. When done, return to your original station.

Why do you think there are four different stations?

_____

_____

**STEP 2**  Find your station below, and complete step 2 for that station.

- **Hillside model:**  Use a small stack of thin books to slowly elevate the height of the sandy end of the cookie sheet. Watch the sand. When it begins to slide downhill, record the height of the higher end of the cookie sheet. Leave the cookie sheet in that position so other groups can observe the same results.

- **Sand dune model:**  Turn on the lowest speed of the fan at one end of the cookie sheet, and observe what happens. Record your observations in the data table. Turn off the fan and leave the model so other groups can record their observations.

- **Glacier model:**  Use a book to gently prop up the end of the cookie sheet nearest the ice cube. Firmly press the ice against the clay and slowly slide it down the slope. Record your observations in the data table. Leave the model alone so other groups can record their observations.

- **Beaver dam model:**  Use the wooden stirrer or alternate materials to build a beaver dam across the middle of the river. Be sure that the dam is relatively watertight. Slowly add water to the river on just one side of the dam and observe what happens. Record your observations. Leave the model alone so other groups can record their observations.

**STEP 3** Rotate through the stations again, recording your observations. Compare your observations and experiences with the models as a class, and revise your data table, if needed.

List your comparisons below. How were your observations similar and different?

_____

_____

_____

_____

| Model | Initial observations | Observations after change |
|---|---|---|
| Hillside | | |
| Sand dunes | | |
| Glacier | | |
| Beaver dam | | |

## Analyze Your Results

**STEP 4** Describe the changes to Earth's surface you modeled in this activity. Include the forces that caused these changes in your descriptions. Use the terms *weathering, erosion,* or *deposition* and other terms if they fit your results.

_____

_____

_____

_____

_____

_____

_____

## Draw Conclusions

**STEP 5** How could you modify one of the setups in this activity to model how earthquakes can trigger erosion? Suggest one modification of materials and one modification of how you physically handle the model.

_____

_____

_____

**STEP 6** Make a claim about factors that change Earth's surface.

_____

_____

Cite evidence from the models to support your claim.

_____

_____

**STEP 7** Think of other questions you would like to ask about factors that change Earth's surface.

_____

_____

# Always Changing

## Evidence of Change

The different processes you've learned about that change Earth's surface are happening all around the world. Some of these processes occur quickly, and others happen slowly. Explore the illustrated environments on this page and the next.

Desert Oasis

Explore Online

**20.** Observe and record the changes that have occurred and are occurring above. Include the force that caused the change.

| Image | What's happening |
|---|---|
| **a.** Mushroom rock | |
| **b.** Plant roots | |
| **c.** Waterfall | |
| **d.** Rocks at base of slope | |
| **e.** Digging animal | |

# Forces in the Cold

Weathering occurs in cold places just as it does in warm places. Glaciers can move along the land, scraping up and grinding dirt and rock. Water can seep into rocks, freeze, melt, and freeze again until the rocks break apart.

21. Observe the image for signs of weathering, erosion, and deposition in the environment below.

▷ **Explore Online**

22. Use your observations to complete the table below. One has been done for you.

| Image | What's Happening |
|---|---|
| **a.** Glacier | |
| **b.** Moraine | A previous glacier moved rock and deposited it here as the glacier melted. |
| **c.** Beach | |
| **d.** Cracked rock | |

 **EVIDENCE NOTEBOOK** What similarities can you find in both tables? Make a list in your Evidence Notebook.

© Houghton Mifflin Harcourt

**23.** Look at the images below. Determine the cause and effect for each change shown. Some may have more than one cause or effect. Then give evidence for your answers.

▷ **Explore Online**

**Causes:** gravity     wind     water     plant growth    ice

**Effects:** weathering    erosion    deposition

Cause:_____

_____

Effects:_____

_____

Evidence:_____

_____

_____

Cause:_____

_____

Effects:_____

_____

Evidence:_____

_____

_____

Cause:_____

_____

Effects:_____

_____

Evidence:_____

_____

_____

## Do the Math

## A Waterfall Over Time

**24.** It took one year for 2 cm of rock to erode under a waterfall. Look at the table to see the effect of the waterfall over time. Fill in the table for the unknown amount of erosion.

| 2 years | 50 years | 100 years | 1,000 years | 10,000 years |
|---------|----------|-----------|-------------|--------------|
| 4 cm | 100 cm | | | |

 **EVIDENCE NOTEBOOK** Think about all the ways the surface features of the desert environment changed. Consider which of those are similar to the rock you saw at the beginning of the lesson. List the causes in two columns titled: *Could have formed the rock* and *Could not have formed the rock.*

## Putting It Together

**25.** Complete the sentences in the paragraph by selecting the correct words.

> **icebergs**  **glaciers**  **clouds**
>
> **erosion**  **weathering**  **deposition**
>
> **rockslide**  **waves**  **sandstorm**

In cold locations, the slow downhill movement of large

_____ can erode the rock and sediment. In the same

locations, the cycle of freezing and thawing in cracked rocks is

a cause of _____. If enough rocks build up on a hill,

they may tumble down as a _____. The burrowing of

animals causes _____ and _____.

Liquid water in the form of waterfalls, rivers, rain, and

_____ can cause erosion.

# Discover More

**Check out this path . . . or go online to choose one of these other paths.**

| Seeking Stability | • **Extremes!**<br>• **The Science of Slopes** |

## No Disruptions

**Engineer It!**

# Slowing Change

Floods, landslides, and other changes to Earth's surface can disrupt people's lives.

Engineers try to prevent some of these disruptions by designing and building structures such as wind barriers, levees, and sand fences. People can also help prevent erosion on hills by planting grasses, shrubs, and trees.

Look at the images here and on the next page. Then read about some of the ways engineers try to prevent disruptions.

Levees are long embankments or mounds of dirt along rivers or waterways that help prevent flooding.

Wind barriers are rows of trees that help prevent erosion by providing a natural barrier to blowing wind.

399

Sand fences are used to force blowing sand to accumulate in a certain place. This helps prevent erosion of the sand.

Rooted plants help prevent topsoil erosion caused by wind or running water after rain or a storm.

**26.** Research one of the changes you've learned about in this lesson, such as erosion of beaches or rockslides. Come up with a plan to help prevent that change. Use the table below to describe your plan and list its pros and cons.

| Plan |
| --- |
|  |
| **Pros** |
|  |
| **Cons** |
|  |

# Lesson Check

Name _____

## Can You Explain It?

Explore Online

1. Now that you've learned more about other factors that shape Earth's surface, explain how this rock formed. Be sure to do the following:

   • Describe what the rock probably looked like before it changed.

   • Explain what forces shaped the rock, and how much time they probably took.

   • Predict what might happen to the rock in the future, and how.

   • Use the terms *erosion, weathering,* and *deposition* in your answer.

**EVIDENCE NOTEBOOK** Use the information you've collected in your Evidence Notebook to help you cover each point above.

_____

_____

_____

_____

_____

_____

_____

_____

## Checkpoints

2. Which of the following is both a product of weathering and a factor that causes weathering?

   **a.** gravity          **c.** wind

   **b.** water           **d.** sand

Circle the correct answer or answers to each question below.

**3.** Which of the following factors contribute to weathering of rock?
   **a.** prairie dog digging burrows in the soil of a grassland
   **b.** the cycle of water freezing and thawing in cracks of exposed rock
   **c.** gravity causing rocks to tumble off cliffs or down hillsides
   **d.** a beaver building a dam across a stream
   **e.** plant roots growing into cracks of a cliff wall

**4.** Which of the following can be factors in weathering, erosion, and deposition. Choose all that apply.
   **a.** sand
   **c.** ice
   **b.** wind
   **d.** clouds

**5.** Which of the following most likely is not evidence of deposition?
   **a.** Damp sediment is piled up at the base of a mountain after the snow has melted.
   **b.** A river delta is broader and its water murkier after a flash flood has occurred upriver.
   **c.** A hiker finds small, flat rocks stacked at the peak of a mountain.
   **d.** A beach appears to have more sand after a large ocean storm.

**6.** Write the eight different terms to fill out four different sequences that begin with extreme events and cause changes to Earth's surface.

| deposition of sand in city | earthquake | erosion of riverbanks | flash flood |
| hurricane | large waves | loosened sediment | strong winds in desert |

| | | | | |
|---|---|---|---|---|
| | → | | → | beach erosion |
| severe rain storm | → | | → | |
| | → | sandstorm | → | |
| | → | | → | erosion of hillsides |

# Lesson Roundup

**A.** In the space below, describe how plants and animals can cause weathering or erosion. Give a real example of each organism and how it causes weathering or erosion.

_____

_____

_____

_____

· · · · · · · · · · · · · · · · · · · · · · · · · · · · · · · · · · · · · · · · · · · · · · · · · · · · · · · · · · · · · ·

**B.** Write the correct words to complete the paragraph.

A hillside in a tropical rain forest is likely to have more erosion

from _____ than a desert because of the difference

in _____. A desert is likely to have more erosion from

_____ than a tropical rain forest because desert

landscapes are more exposed. In many environments, plants prevent

_____ by holding soil, rocks, and sediment in place with

their roots. However, plants can cause _____ when their

_____ grow and expand inside cracks of rocks.

> water
> wind
> rainfall
> temperature
> deposition
> weathering
> erosion
> trunks
> leaves
> roots

· · · · · · · · · · · · · · · · · · · · · · · · · · · · · · · · · · · · · · · · · · · · · · · · · · · · · · · · · · · · · ·

**C.** Circle the process or processes happening in each image.

**flood**

weathering,
erosion,
deposition

**ivy**

weathering,
erosion,
deposition

**delta**

weathering,
erosion,
deposition

**meerkat**

weathering,
erosion,
deposition

**403**

# How Can Maps Help Us Learn About Earth's Surface?

Earth has many landforms such as mountains, valleys, and plains. Maps can model the surface features of Earth. Lines on a map can show the shape of the land. Numbers on the lines tell how high or low the land is.

**By the end of this lesson . . .**
you'll be able to use maps to learn about Earth's features.

# Can You Explain It?

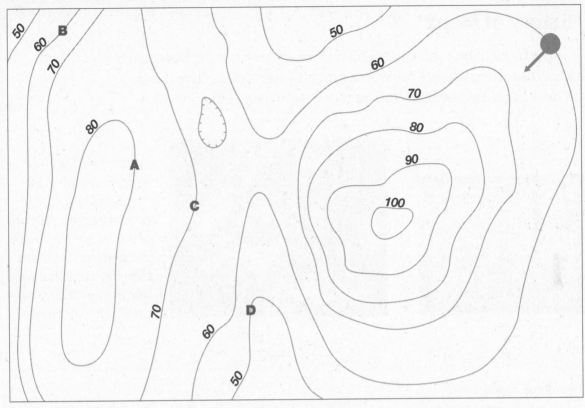

This is a topographic map. The lines and numbers tell the shape of the land.

**1.** Imagine standing at the placed marked by the red dot. What would you see if you looked in the direction of the arrow? How can you tell?

_____

_____

_____

_____

_____

 **EVIDENCE NOTEBOOK** Look for this icon to help you gather evidence to answer the questions above.

# What Is a Map?

## A History of Maps

If you wanted to go somewhere you had never been before, how would you know how to get there? You would probably use a map. Over time, maps have been used by many different people in many different ways.

Photos taken from airplanes allowed for more accurate, or correct, representations of distances. They were better representations than the maps that were drawn from an on-the-ground perspective.

Hundreds of years ago, people walked the land or sailed the coast and drew what they saw to capture the overall shape of a place. The maps showed important roads, areas, landforms, and bodies of waters. The measurements were not always very accurate.

Printed road maps show not only major roads but also less traveled minor roads. Maps are changed and reprinted as new roads are constructed. Before smartphones or GPS, a family driving across the United States would carry a road map.

2. What is a disadvantage of a printed road map?

   a. Printed road maps cannot be used without a smartphone or GPS.

   b. They only show major roads and aren't very detailed.

   c. Printed road maps can be carried from place to place.

   d. When new roads are constructed or old roads are removed, a new road map needs to be printed.

Satellites in space take photographs of locations all around Earth. This provides more detail of the area and can be sent electronically for use.

Global Positioning System (GPS) technology uses information from satellites. The GPS picks up information from satellites and uses it to determine your position on Earth. Using a map like this shows you exactly where you are while you are traveling.

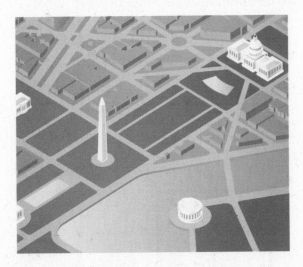

A 3D map shows the height and shape of land, buildings, and other features in a realistic way . Some 3D models are drawn by people with help from computers. There are also satellites that can record and analyze different images and piece them together into accurate 3D maps that a user can "fly through" on a computer or mobile device.

**3.** What are the benefits of using GPS? Circle all the answers that apply.

    **a.** It shows exactly where you are.

    **b.** It uses a 3D model.

    **c.** It can be used on a smartphone.

    **d.** It is very accurate.

# How Many Maps

Different maps show different things. You choose a map depending on what you want to use it for. Explore the images to learn more about different types of maps.

**4.** What kind of maps have you used?

_____

_____

_____

**Weather maps** show rainfall, temperature, air pressure, and other types of weather. Data from satellites and tools on Earth's surface are used to make weather maps.

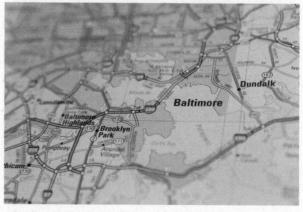

A **road map** shows all kinds of roads—from major to minor roads. When driving in a new area, road maps can help people figure out the best way to get to their destination.

**Locator maps**, such as this shopping mall map, help you find your way around a place. A *You Are Here* marker shows where you are standing compared to the rest of the mall stores. This way you can figure out how to get to certain stores.

A **floor plan** shows the relationship of the rooms in a building. It may show closets, doors, windows, and bedrooms. This map could help people who are looking for a new home figure out if the house has the features they need.

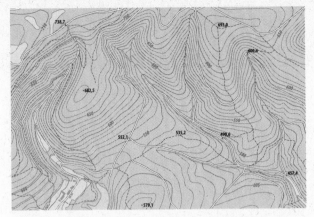

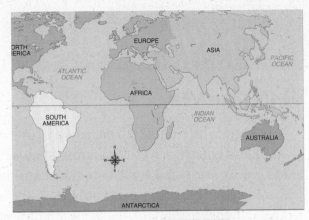

A **topographic map** shows features such as mountains or waterways. The features can be natural or human-made. Contour lines reveal the height and distances of these features in relation to each other.

A **world map** shows the **continents,** which are the major landmasses on Earth, and the oceans. Other features might be shown on a world map, too, such as country boundaries, islands, lakes, and mountains.

 5. **Language SmArts** Compare and contrast two different maps on this spread.

_____

_____

_____

 6. Which type of map would be the most helpful when going on vacation? Why?

_____

**EVIDENCE NOTEBOOK** Which type of map gives information most like the one you saw at the beginning of this lesson? What kinds of information does that type of map provide? Record your findings in your Evidence Notebook.

## Putting It Together

7. Complete the sentences by choosing the best words or phrases.

| features |
| materials |
| road |
| 3D |
| weather |
| locator |
| topographic |
| GPS |

Maps represent Earth's _____. People use different

maps for different needs. A _____ map shows

how and where it is raining or snowing. A _____

map helps people get from one store to another store in a mall.

Signals that travel from a satellite to a smartphone are used to

show your place on a _____ map.

# How Do You Read a Map?

## Find Your Way

Knowing which direction on a map points north lets you use the map to find your way. A compass rose shows the cardinal directions—north, south, east, and west. Often the cardinal directions are indicated on the compass rose as N, S, E, and W. The points shown between two directions are called intercardinal directions. For example the mark between north and west is the northwest direction.

**compass rose**

### A Map of Washington, D.C.

Use the compass rose and the map of Washington, D.C. to answer the questions.

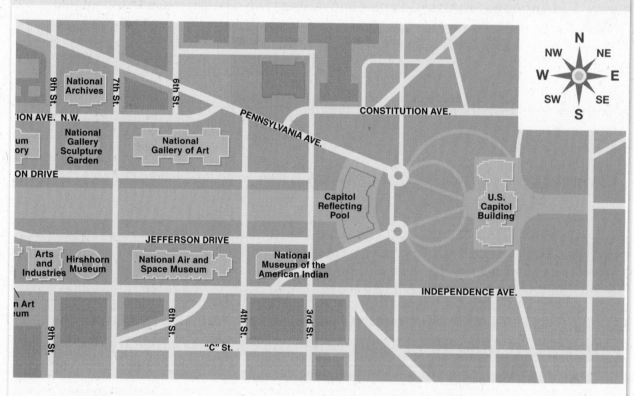

8. In what direction must you move from the intersection of Pennsylvania Avenue and 6th Street to get to the U.S. Capitol Building?
   a. north
   b. northeast
   c. east
   d. southeast

9. Starting at the Hirshhorn Museum, travel east along Jefferson Drive. Turn north on 3rd Street, and look to the east. What do you see?
   a. National Gallery of Art
   b. National Air and Space Museum
   c. Constitution Avenue
   d. Capitol Reflecting Pool

## It's Key!

An important part of any map is the key, or tool to unlock what the map shows. The key explains the meaning of the map's symbols, colors, and lines.

**10.** Why is a map key important?

_____

_____

_____

**11.** How many lakes on the map are located within the state of Nevada? Do not count lakes that border the state.

**a.** 1      **b.** 3      **c.** 5      **d.** 12

## World Climate

**12.** This map shows Earth's climate. Use the key to answer the questions. Place an "x" on all the polar climates.

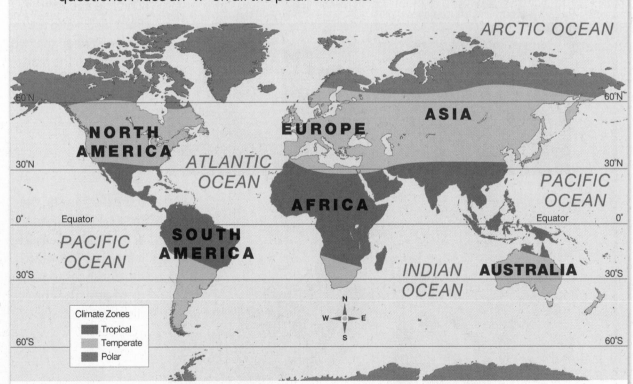

**13.** What climate zones are found in Australia? Circle all correct answers.

     **a.** polar      **b.** tropical      **c.** pacific      **d.** temperate

# Do the Math
## Using a Map Scale

▷ **Explore Online**

Maps can be as small as the screen on a smartphone or as big as a dining room table. Most maps have a **scale**. The scale relates the distance on the map to the distance on Earth. Read below to learn how to use a map scale.

**a.**

Using the edge of a blank sheet of paper, copy the scale off the map.

**b.**

Use the scale you copied to find the distance between Chicago and Detroit. Start by placing the scale between the two city dots on the map. The distance from Chicago to Detroit is 450 km.

**c.**

If the distance on the map is longer than the actual scale, measure it in parts. Then add the distances together to arrive at the correct distance.

412

**14.** For some printed maps, you can use a ruler as a scale. In the scale below 1 cm on the map is equal to 5 km on Earth. Multiply to find out the distances in kilometers.

**Rule: 1 cm = 5 km**

| Measure | Distance | | | | | | |
|---------|---|---|---|---|---|---|---|
| cm | 1 | 2 | 3 | 4 | 5 | 6 | 7 |
| km | 5 | 10 | | | | | |

**15.** The map below shows the state of Montana. The map scale shows the scaled distance on the map. Find the cities Big Timber and Roundup in the central, southern part of this state. The distance from the city Big Timber to Roundup is about 120 km. Try measuring it yourself. Then, work with a partner to find two cities that are about 60 km apart.

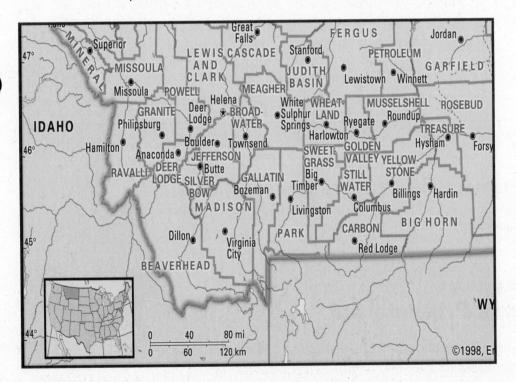

**16.** Pick two cities on the map, and measure their distances using the map scale.

## Make a Map

**17.** Draw a map of your school, including a map key that would help a map reader identify key features of the school, such as exits, water fountains, offices, and so on.

**EVIDENCE NOTEBOOK** Think about the different features of maps, such as keys and scale. In your Evidence Notebook, record how these features can be used to read a map.

**Language SmArts**
## Make a Presentation

**18.** Make a digital presentation that shows how to use a key, scale, and compass rose to read a map. List the parts of your presentation below.

_____

_____

_____

_____

# What Can Maps Show Us?

## It's On the Map!

You have learned about different types of maps, keys, compass roses, and scales. Now you will learn how scientists use maps to study Earth. View the different maps for details about each map.

**Medical Map** Scientists use these maps to identify patterns, such as locations where certain diseases are more common.

**Weather Map** This map shows rainfall, temperature, air pressure, and other parts of weather. A weather map usually applies to a few days.

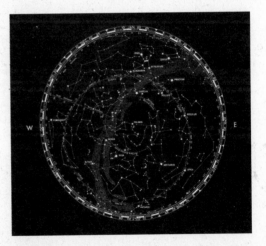

**Resource Map** This map shows where resources such as gold, iron, and coal are found. Maps such as these help scientists determine patterns of where specific resources may be located.

**Star Map** This map shows the positions of some of the stars and planets in the night sky. Star maps help scientists point their telescopes in the direction of the objects they want to observe.

**19.** What other ways do you think scientists use maps?

_____

_____

_____

# How High?

A topographic map uses contour lines to show a mountain's change in elevation. **Elevation** is the height above or below the level of the sea. The contour lines are marked in equal elevations on the map. The closer the lines are drawn , the steeper the mountain is.

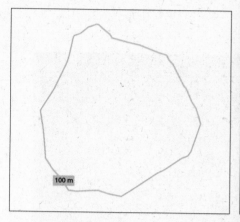

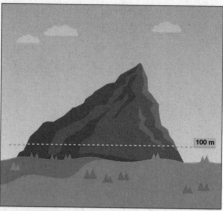

To make a topographic map of this mountain, we will begin by drawing the first contour line at 100 meters. The shape of the line shows the shape of the mountain at the given elevation.

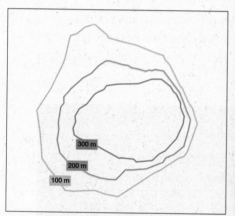

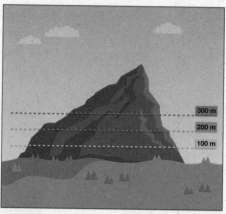

The shape of the mountain is marked every 100 meters as the elevation rises. Notice that the bands are drawn closer together on the right side and wider on the left. Discuss with a partner why it is drawn this way.

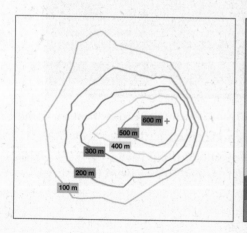

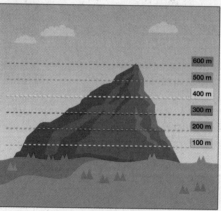

The contour lines continue every 100 meters until the summit, or the highest point of the mountain, is reached. The summit is shown with a cross. How can you tell by looking at the map, which side of the mountain is the steepest?

Topographic maps are useful for planning buildings and roads. They have other uses too, such as for hiking.

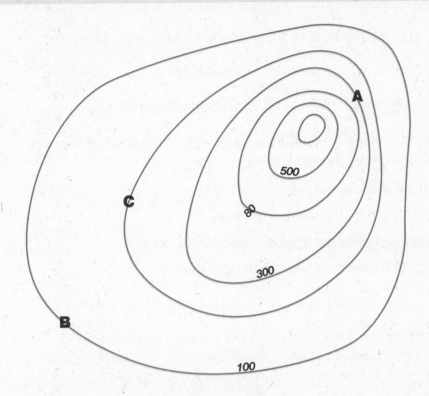

**20.** A group of hikers is planning to climb the mountain shown on the map. They would like to climb the part of the mountain that is the least steep. How should they plan their climb?

   **a.** Start below area B, then continue through area C to the top.

   **b.** Start below area A, then climb up through area A to the top.

   **c.** Start below area B, then cross to area A, and continue to the top.

   **d.** Start below area A, then cross to area C, and continue to the top.

**21.** Which of these points on the map has the highest elevation?

   **a.** A

   **b.** B

   **c.** C

**22.** Write the words that complete the sentences.

| topographic | resource | star |
|---|---|---|
| weather | medical | world |

Maps provide many different kinds of useful information.

A _____ map is used to show where it is raining. To study the

night sky, use a _____ map. Scientists use _____

maps to identify patterns of the flu or other diseases in an area.

**23.** How can you tell how steep a mountain is by looking at the contour lines on a topographic map? Circle the best answer.

**a.** The higher the elevation, the steeper the area.

**b.** The lower the elevation, the steeper the area.

**c.** The more space between the lines, the steeper the area.

**d.** The less space between the lines, the steeper the area.

 **EVIDENCE NOTEBOOK** What do the lines and numbers on a topographic map indicate? What does it mean when the lines are close together or far apart? Record your answers to these questions in your Evidence Notebook.

 Language SmArts
# Use Reasons and Evidence

**24.** You are planning a road trip across the country to do some hiking. What types of maps will be useful for your trip? Support your choices with reasons why you've chosen these maps.

_____

_____

_____

_____

_____

_____

_____

**Tip**

The English Language Arts Handbook can provide help with understanding how to use reason and evidence.

# Park Designer

## Objective

**Collaborate** to design a park. A park designer uses a map to plan where equipment and features go in the park. Think about how a park designer uses a map to do his or her job.

**Find a Problem:** What question will you investigate to meet this objective?

---

---

### Materials

- printed park site map
- printed park material cutouts
- ruler
- glue
- scissors
- notebook

## Procedure

**STEP 1  Brainstorm:** With your group, read through the criteria and constraints for this project. Brainstorm ideas with your group on how you can build the park and follow the requirements.

Think about the features in your park. To be successful, your park will meet certain criteria and constraints:

### Criteria

- ☐ Include a playground area.
- ☐ Include an eating area.
- ☐ Include ways to protect the animals that live in and around the lake, such as ducks, raccoons, fish, and bats.
- ☐ Include several rest areas spread out in the park.

### Constraints

- ☐ Your park can cost no more than $7,000.
- ☐ Allow 90 centimeters minimum walking space between objects that people must walk around.
- ☐ Include a 240 × 240 cm garden.

**STEP 2 Plan:** First, talk with your group about ideas that were brainstormed, and select those that seem most successful. Then, start drawing a rough draft of your park's design. Do not spend too much time on details. Last, make sure you are in budget by listing the items you need and the cost.

**STEP 3 Build:** Begin building your park on the provided map. Cut and lay out all your pieces first. Once you are happy with the placement, glue the pieces down. Use the scale to measure distances to be sure you meet the criteria and constraints. Make sure you add a key.

**STEP 4 Evaluate and Redesign:** Check to make sure you have met the criteria and the constraints. You might change your map several times before you have the most successful plan.

## Analyze Your Results

**STEP 5** How could you redesign the park at a lower cost?

_____

_____

_____

_____

**STEP 6** How does your park's design allow for the survival of the animals that live in and around the lake?

_____

_____

_____

_____

**STEP 7** How did you make sure there was enough walking space for getting around the entire park?

_____

_____

_____

_____

## Draw Conclusions

**STEP 8** **Communicate:** Compare your park with your classmates' parks. Name one thing you designed well and explain why you think so. Name one thing another group did well and explain why you think so.

_____

_____

_____

_____

**STEP 9** In your opinion, what part or area of your park would you like to change? Why?

_____

_____

_____

_____

**STEP 10** Make a claim based on your investigation. Cite evidence from the activity to support your claim.

_____

_____

_____

**STEP 11** Think of other questions you have about designing maps.

_____

_____

# Discover More

**Check out this path . . . or go online to choose one of these other paths.**

**Careers in Science and Engineering**

• **Search Party**
• **Above and Below**

## City Planner

To build a park, you would have worked with a city planner. City planners plan out city lands to suit the needs of the people living there.

City planners need to work and communicate well with others. They approve or deny plans to build in the city. They meet with the residents of the city, lawyers, builders, and politicians to decide what is best for the city.

City planners should have a good understanding of maps to help plan the layout of the city. Specific parts of land may be zoned, or set aside, for houses, businesses, retail stores, roads, public parks, and schools.

City planners must plan solutions to traffic and transportation problems. Buses and trains help reduce traffic and pollution in growing cities.

City planners help make laws about how land can be used. They make decisions about requirements for new buildings. For example, in an area with hurricanes, they may require buildings to withstand high winds.

City planners also must consider how to conserve, or protect, spaces for the local wildlife and plants. They may set aside a wooded area that cannot be developed or require a certain number of parks be built to preserve nature.

**25.** How do city planners use science and engineering in their job?

_____

_____

**26.** Suppose you want to add a new park to your city. You will have to decide what part of the city you can replace with a park. Do research to locate and print a map of your town. Use that map as a guide to draw a new map below that includes the location of your new park. Then answer the questions below.

**27.** About how big is the park you added? How did you decide on its size?

_____

_____

_____

_____

**28.** What did you remove to make room for the park? Does this change cause other problems? If you were the city planner, how would you solve them?

_____

_____

_____

_____

# Lesson Check

Name _____

## Can You Explain It?

1. Review the topographic map from the beginning of the lesson. What does it show? Summarize what maps show and how they are useful. Be sure to include the following:

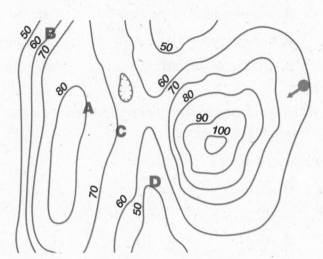

- Names and descriptions of different types of maps.

- Features that help you interpret a map's contents.

- Descriptions of how maps can be used.

📖 **EVIDENCE NOTEBOOK** Use the information you've collected in your Evidence Notebook to help you cover each point above.

_____

_____

_____

_____

_____

_____

_____

_____

_____

## Checkpoints

2. How are maps useful to scientists in their work?
   a. Maps can be used to show data about weather or resources to make predictions.
   b. Maps can be used to show the location of rooms in a building.
   c. Maps can be used to show the state capital cities.
   d. Maps can be used to show the order of steps in an experiment.

**Answer each question below about maps and their uses.**

3. Different maps show different kinds of information. Circle all the kinds of information a map can show.

   a. the elevation of the land

   b. the life cycle of a butterfly

   c. the location of stores

   d. the way to put together parts of a bicycle

   e. the way a rainbow forms

   f. the distance between two cities

4. What is the change in elevation between point B and point D?

   a. 10 m

   b. 20 m

   c. 30 m

   d. 40 m

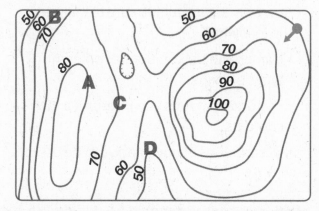

5. What is the capital of Nevada?

   a. Tonopah

   b. Carson City

   c. Las Vegas

   d. Wells

6. About how far across is the state of Nevada at its widest part?

   a. 100 km

   b. 300 km

   c. 500 km

   d. 600 km

©1998, Encyclopædia Britannica, Inc.

# Lesson Roundup

**A.** Today, maps often show satellite images with roads or other kinds of information on them. Which of the following most likely describes a map from 250 years ago? Circle the correct answer.

    **a.** a printed road map showing large highways

    **b.** a 3D map showing all of the buildings in a city

    **c.** a computer map showing large and small roads

    **d.** a hand-drawn map showing the main roads in a town

**B.** Draw a line from each map part to match the correct description of how it is used.

**a figure on a map that is used to show which way is north, south, east, and west**

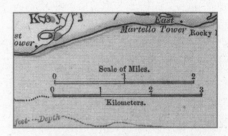

**a figure on a map that shows the relationship between distances on the map and the distances on Earth's surface.**

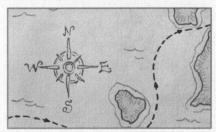

**a figure on a map that explains the meaning of the map's symbols, colors, and lines**

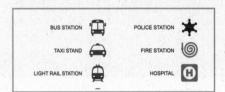

**C.** What else did you learn about the parts of a map?

_____

_____

_____

_____

_____

# What Patterns Do Maps Show Us?

An erupting volcano is a spectacular sight, especially at night. Volcanoes form when pressure below Earth's surface causes hot, melted rock called *lava* to flow onto the land. They also form when ash explodes onto Earth's surface. Volcanoes are found only in certain places on Earth. Do you know where?

**By the end of this lesson . . .**

you'll be able to describe patterns about the locations of earthquakes, volcanoes, mountains, and ocean trenches.

© Houghton Mifflin Harcourt • Image Credits: ©Paul A. Souders/Digital Vision/Getty Images

# Can You Explain It?

Great Rift Valley

N W E S

km 0    400
mi 0    400

In 2005, a huge crack began to form in the desert of eastern Africa. This giant crack is part of the Rift Valley. A rift is a large crack in Earth's surface where the top layers of Earth are being pulled apart.

1. The rift in Africa is getting bigger and deeper every year. Study the map. Predict how the land and bodies of water in this area of the world might change as the rift changes.

_____

_____

_____

_____

_____

_____

_____

_____

_____

**Tip**

Learn more about processes and things that can change Earth's rocks in What other Factors Shape Earth's Surface?

**EVIDENCE NOTEBOOK**  Look for this icon to help you gather evidence to answer the question above.

# By Land or By Sea

## Ring of Fire

Volcanoes form when lava flows onto Earth's surface. Some volcanoes form on land, some form under water. Earthquakes happen when large blocks of rock shift and release stored energy. Earthquakes happen on land and under water, too, and cause the ground to shake.

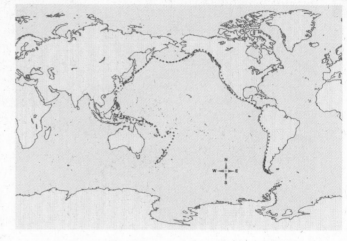

Thankfully, volcanic eruptions and earthquakes do not occur everywhere. But one area of Earth that does experience many volcanoes and earthquakes is along the edges of the Pacific Ocean. This region is called the Ring of Fire. Look at the map to locate this area that rings a large part of the Pacific Ocean.

Now look at the photos below. They are evidence of how earthquakes and volcanoes can change Earth's surface.

Earthquakes occur on land and under water. On land, they can cause the ground to crack.

The shaking of the ground during an earthquake can cause much damage. Sometimes, it makes buildings collapse.

Volcanoes can send lava, ash, smoke, and dust high into the air. Eruptions also add dangerous gases to the air.

Some volcanoes form tall mountains as the lava and other erupted materials cool and build up over time.

**2. Language SmArts** Compare and contrast earthquakes and volcanoes.

_____

_____

_____

**3.** Complete the sentences.

The Ring of Fire is an area with many _____ and _____.

It is located around the _____.

**4.** Which are true of volcanoes? Circle all that apply.

   **a.** They always form tall mountains.

   **b.** They can pollute the air.

   **c.** Many form in the Ring of Fire.

   **d.** They cause the ground to crack.

 **HANDS-ON  Apply What You Know**

# Earthquakes and Buildings

Earthquakes can cause much damage to buildings. Work with two or three others to design and test a building that will survive a model earthquake.

**Materials**
- toothpicks
- modeling clay
- 2 desks or tables
- stopwatch

## Procedure

**1.** With your team, brainstorm for 2 minutes to come up with a possible toothpick-clay building design. One design constraint is that the structure must be 4 stories high; 1 toothpick length equals 1 story height. Sketch your team's design on paper.

**2.** Construct your model building in 5 minutes or less.

**3.** Test your design, placing it over the space between two desks pushed together. Gently shake the desks or tables for 1 minute to simulate an earthquake.

**4.** With your team, spend 3 minutes discussing how well your design withstood the earthquake. Identify two or three ways to improve your design.

 **EVIDENCE NOTEBOOK**  Do any of the images remind you of the African Rift? How does this help you begin to understand what is happening in the Rift Valley?

# Up and Down

Other features that can be found on Earth's surface are mountains and trenches. Study the drawing as you read about these two features of Earth's surface.

## Mountains and Trenches

**5.** Use the information below to label the image. You may use a word more than once.

| mountains |
| trench |

This drawing shows some land and ocean features. Drawing is not to scale.

 Mountains can form on land. Some are very tall and jagged, while others are smaller and rounded. Mt. Everest in the Himalayan Mountains is the tallest mountain on land. It is 8,848 meters high.

Mountains form under water, too. A huge mountain range called the Mid-Atlantic Ridge runs down the middle of the Atlantic Ocean.

 An **ocean trench** is a long, deep, narrow valley found on the ocean floor. The Marianas Trench in the Pacific Ocean is the deepest known part of the ocean. It is more than 10,994 meters deep!

**6.** Which is true of mountains? Circle all that apply.
   **a.** Some are rounded.
   **b.** Some are tall and jagged.
   **c.** They form only under water.
   **d.** They form on land and under water.

**7.** What is an ocean trench?
   **a.** an island that forms in the ocean
   **b.** a volcano with a jagged peak
   **c.** a round mountain on land
   **d.** a deep, narrow valley on the ocean floor

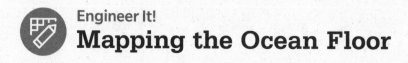

Engineer It!
# Mapping the Ocean Floor

The ocean floor has many interesting features—mountains, trenches, and volcanoes, just to name a few. But how do we know this?

Multibeam sonar is a technology that uses sound waves to determine how deep the ocean floor is. The signal is sent out from a ship in a fan like pattern, and it returns data about the features found on the ocean floor. This information is used to make ocean floor maps.

**8.** How is the ocean floor mapped?

_____

_____

## Putting It Together

**9.** On each line, write whether the feature forms on *land, under water,* or *both*.

**mountains**

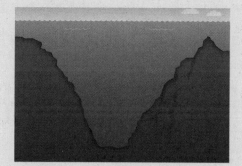

**trench**

**volcano**

**earthquake**

# Can Maps Help Us See Patterns?

## Finding Patterns on Land

You just learned that mountains, earthquakes, and volcanoes can occur in the ocean and on land. Are there particular places on Earth where they are more likely to occur? Look at these maps to help you answer this question.

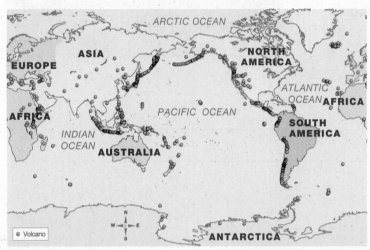

This map shows the locations of volcanoes that have formed on land.

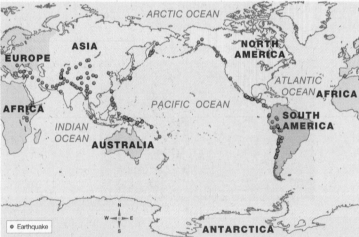

This map shows the locations of earthquakes that have occurred on land.

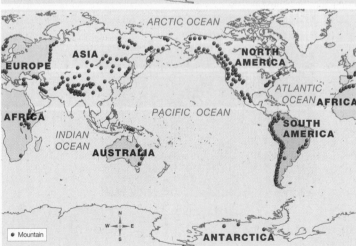

This map shows the locations of mountains that have formed on land.

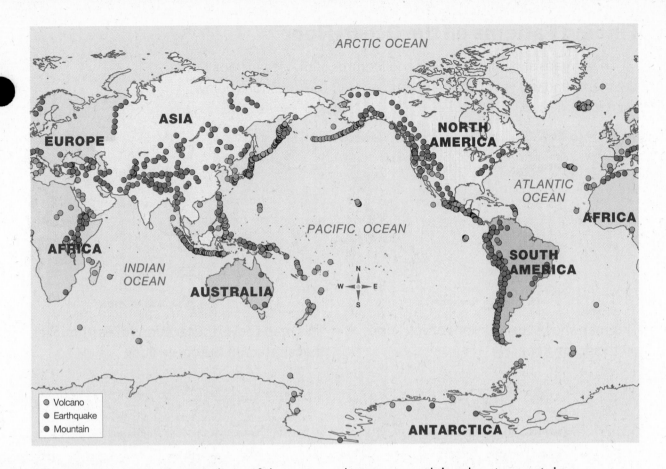

Legend:
- Volcano
- Earthquake
- Mountain

**10.** Based on your observations of the maps, what can you claim about mountains, volcanoes, and earthquakes?

_____

_____

_____

_____

**11.** Choose the words or phrases that correctly complete each sentence

> **in the center**     **near the edges**

Earthquakes on land are most likely to occur _____ of continents.

Volcanoes on land often are located _____ of continents. Mountains

on land are found _____ and _____ of continents.

 **EVIDENCE NOTEBOOK** How can these map patterns help you predict what is happening in the African Rift Valley?

# Finding Patterns on the Ocean Floor

These maps show earthquakes and features of the ocean floor. Study the maps, and use your observations to answer the questions below.

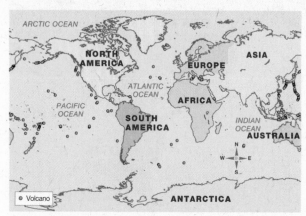

This map shows the locations of volcanoes on the ocean floor.

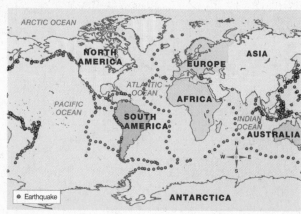

This map shows the locations of earthquakes that started on the ocean floor.

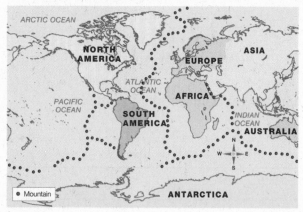

This map shows the mountains on the ocean floor.

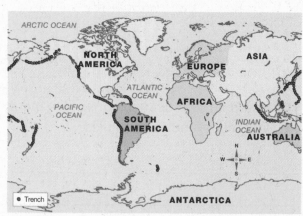

This map shows trenches on the ocean floor.

**12.** Describe the pattern of ocean trenches.

_____

_____

_____

**13.** Choose the words or phrases that correctly complete each sentence.

> **the centers of oceans**    **coastlines**    **islands**

Most underwater volcanoes occur near _____, and a few occur in the

middle. Many underwater mountain ranges are found near _____.

Ocean trenches are common near _____.

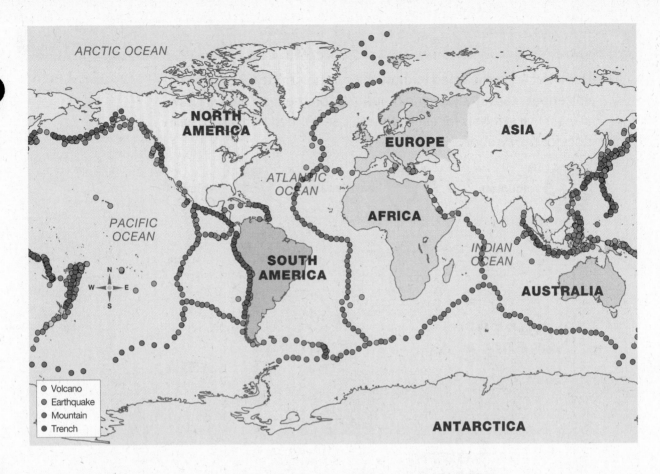

**14.** Compare the locations of earthquakes and volcanoes on land and the ocean floor. Use the map from the previous pages to compare.

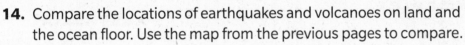
_____
_____
_____

**15.** Contrast the locations of mountain ranges on land and the ocean floor. Use the map from the previous pages to compare.

_____
_____
_____

**16.** Use what you've learned to draw the symbols for the locations of volcanoes, earthquakes, and mountains on the map below. Draw at least five symbols for each feature. Use colored pencils to make dots for the symbols.

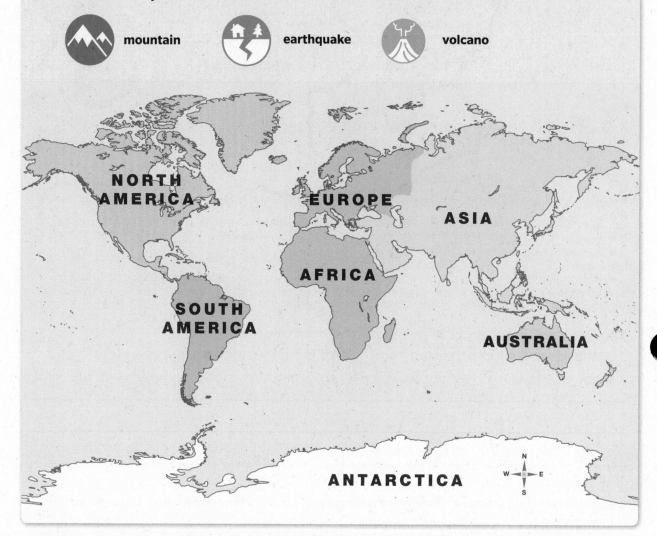

 **HANDS-ON Apply What You Know**

## Modeling Features of the Ocean Floor

**17.** Use modeling clay to make a 3D model of the features of the ocean floor. Include locations of volcanoes, mountains, trenches, and earthquakes. Label your model.

**18.** How would you describe the location of most underwater mountain ranges?

   **a.** They are at the edges of continents.

   **b.** They are usually in the middle of oceans.

   **c.** They are usually near large islands.

   **d.** They are always near the equator.

**19.** Where would volcanoes be most common?

   **a.** the central part of Asia

   **b.** the edges of the Pacific Ocean

   **c.** the North Pole

   **d.** the edges of the Atlantic Ocean

**20.** What is true of earthquakes?

   **a.** They only happen on land.

   **b.** Most happen at the edge of the Atlantic Ocean.

   **c.** They do not occur in any pattern.

   **d.** Many occur near volcanoes.

**21.** What is true of ocean trenches?

   **a.** They look exactly like underwater mountains.

   **b.** They are found in areas where water is shallow.

   **c.** They do not occur in any pattern.

   **d.** They are mostly found near the edges of oceans.

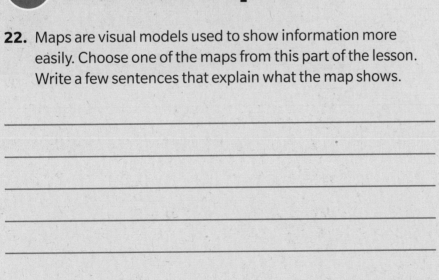

**Language SmArts**

## Understand Graphics

The English Language Arts Handbook can provide help with how to understand graphics.

**22.** Maps are visual models used to show information more easily. Choose one of the maps from this part of the lesson. Write a few sentences that explain what the map shows.

_____

_____

_____

_____

_____

_____

© Houghton Mifflin Harcourt

# Tracking Quakes

In this lesson, you learned that earthquakes happen all over the world. But they usually happen in predictable places. Now you have the chance to look for patterns with real earthquakes.

**Materials**
- world map with country boundaries
- data on earthquakes
- data table
- pencil

## Objective

**Collaborate** to examine data to find out where most earthquakes occur. Scientists detect about 50 earthquakes each day. Most are mild and do not cause any damage, but they occur in the same *type* of area.

What question will you investigate to meet this objective?

_____

_____

## Procedure

**STEP 1** With a partner, find data on 20 earthquakes that have occurred during the past week.

How did you decide which earthquakes to research?

_____

_____

_____

_____

**STEP 2** For each of the 20 earthquakes, record the date, the magnitude, and the location. Use additional paper as needed.

What does a quake's magnitude indicate? Research the term, if needed.

_____

_____

_____

_____

_____

_____

| Earthquakes—Week of _____ | | |
|---|---|---|
| Date | Earthquake magnitude | Location (city or country) |
| | | |
| | | |
| | | |
| | | |
| | | |
| | | |
| | | |
| | | |
| | | |
| | | |

## Analyze Your Results

**STEP 3** Plot the earthquake locations on your world map. You should have one symbol for each location of an earthquake. In which part of the world did most of the earthquakes occur? Did you see a pattern in the location of the earthquakes?

_____

_____

**STEP 4** Of the earthquakes you plotted, in what type of area did most occur?

_____

_____

**STEP 5** Compile the entire class's results into one large data table. Each group should graph the results. What patterns do you see now, and how are those patterns different from the ones above? Did having more data help you see the patterns more clearly?

_____

_____

_____

_____

## Draw Conclusions

**STEP 6** Make a claim about earthquakes. What evidence do you have that most earthquakes occur in certain parts of the world?

_____

_____

_____

_____

**STEP 7** What other questions do you have about the locations of most earthquakes?

_____

_____

_____

_____

# Discover More

**Check out this path . . . or go online to choose one of these other paths.**

| People in Science & Engineering | • Volcano Formation<br>• Volcanic Islands |
| --- | --- |

## Lewis and Clark

▷ **Explore Online**

After the United States purchased the Lousiana Territory from the French in 1803, President Thomas Jefferson asked Meriwether Lewis and William Clark to find a water passage through the territory to make trade and commerce easier. The two men were also asked to create maps of the areas they traveled, including mountains and rivers, to make it easier for future explorers to find their way around. Crossing over steep mountains along their journey was quite a challenge.

**Meriwether Lewis and William Clark**

---

 **HANDS-ON  Apply What You Know**

## Making Mountains!

### Procedure

1. Cover the bottom of the plate with a layer of shaving cream about 1 cm thick.
2. Dip the two pieces of cardboard in the bowl of water until they become soft.
3. Place the damp pieces of cardboard next to each other on top of the shaving cream.
4. Slowly push the pieces toward each other. Observe what happens to the cardboard at the edge where they smash together.
5. Draw a picture of your model, and submit it to your teacher.

**Materials**
- paper plate
- shaving cream
- 2 small pieces of corrugated cardboard
- bowl of water

# Rising High

As you saw in the activity, some mountains form when two slabs of rock smash against each other. The edges of each slab crumpled and folded. Such a collision can also shove one slab of rock up over the other. This process produces some of the world's highest mountains.

Earth's crust is made up of plates, or slabs, that are always moving. Sometimes these slabs move toward each other.

When they meet, the slabs push against each other. This creates heat and pressure at the meeting point.

As the slabs continue to push against each other, mountains form and grow taller.

**23.** How do some of the world's highest mountains form?

_____

_____

_____

# Lesson Check

Name _____

## Can You Explain It?

Explore Online ▷

1. Now that you've learned more about the features of Earth's surface, explain what is happening in the African Rift Valley. Be sure to do the following:

- Explain what could have caused this crack.

- Explain how you used patterns to determine what happened here.

- Predict how the crack might change the nearby land over time.

📋 **EVIDENCE NOTEBOOK** Use the information you've collected in your Evidence Notebook to help you cover each point above.

_____

_____

_____

_____

_____

_____

_____

_____

## Checkpoints

2. You learned about several features found on the ocean floor. How do those compare with the ones on land?

   a. All of them are found on land.

   b. Most of them are found on land.

   c. They do not include volcanoes.

   d. They do not include mountains.

**3.** Circle all the features that occur in the ocean.

**a.** mountains

**c.** volcanoes

**b.** ocean trenches

**d.** earthquakes

**4.** Circle the correct answer. Most volcanoes and earthquakes occur

near the _____.

**a.** middle of the Atlantic Ocean

**c.** coastlines of Africa

**b.** near the Ring of Fire

**d.** the center of South America

**5.** Study the map. Which statements describe the information shown?
Circle all that apply.

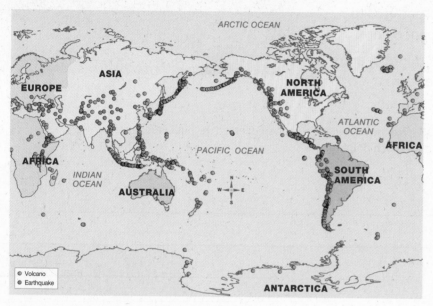

**a.** It shows every volcano on Earth.

**b.** It shows a pattern in the locations of volcanoes.

**c.** It shows where every future earthquake will occur.

**d.** It shows a pattern in the locations of past earthquakes.

**6.** Look at the table. A student used Xs to mark the main locations of features on land.
Some of his answers are incorrect. Help him by circling the correct answers.

| Land patterns | On the edge of continents | In the middle of continents |
|---|---|---|
| earthquake | A) x | |
| volcano | B) x | E) x |
| trench | C) x | |
| mountain | D) x | F) x |

# Lesson Roundup

**A.** What do volcanoes, mountains, and earthquakes have in common?

  **a.** They occur only on land.

  **b.** They occur in areas of the ocean far from land.

  **c.** They occur on land that is far from oceans.

  **d.** They occur on land and in the ocean.

**B.** Imagine you are piloting a submarine just above a somewhat flat area of the ocean floor. The ocean floor begins to slope downward. You cannot see the ocean floor any more. It's as though you've glided off the peak of a steep mountain. A few minutes later, the submarine's sensors tell you the ocean floor is now 5 kilometers deeper than your present depth. What are you and your submarine hovering over?

  **a.** a plain

  **b.** a mountain

  **c.** an ocean trench

  **d.** a volcano

**C.** What does this pattern in the Atlantic Ocean suggest?

  **a.** Slabs of rock are forming walls.

  **b.** The most common place volcanoes occur.

  **c.** Mountains are common between continents.

  **d.** There is an ocean trench between Europe and North America.

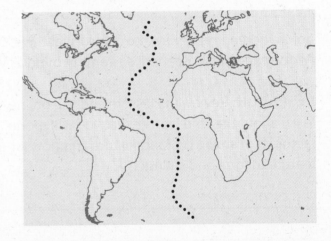

**D.** Why is the pattern shown on the map known as the Ring of Fire?

  **a.** Slabs of smashing rocks cause the Pacific Ocean to warm up.

  **b.** It shows a deep ocean trench, which causes warm water to rise.

  **c.** It is the site of earthquakes caused by volcanoes.

  **d.** It shows volcanoes around the Pacific Ocean.

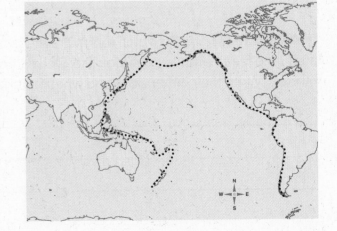

# Model It, Map It

A pair of three-dimensional models can contrast what something looks like before and after a change. Your team will build two models that show how a land feature is changed by wind or water over a long period of time. Then you'll make topographic maps of your models. Your maps' keys will explain the processes that shaped the land features.

Imagine what this land area looked like before the river carved the canyon.

**DEFINE YOUR TASK:** Choose one of these land features to model: a changing coastline, a canyon, a winding river path, or sand dunes. Write a brief description of factors that shape and change that type of land feature.

_____

_____

Before beginning, review the checklist at the end of this Unit Performance Task. Keep those items in mind as you proceed.

**RESEARCH:** Review the lesson, and use online or library resources to learn about the land feature that you will model. Record notes about factors that shape the land feature and how long it takes for such a feature to form and change.

_____

_____

_____

**PLAN YOUR MODELS:** Sketch rough drawings of what your before and after land feature models will look like. Decide how big you will make the models. Write their dimensions and what materials you will use here.

_____

_____

_____

© Houghton Mifflin Harcourt • Image Credits: ©Andresr/Shutterstock

**BUILD YOUR MODELS:** Use materials provided by your teacher to build the before and after models of your selected land feature. Place at least three numbers on parts of each model you will explain in captions.

What features did you number?

_____

_____

_____

**MAP YOUR MODELS:** Draw a topographic map of each model. Make a numbered key for each map. The numbers and features listed on your map key should match the numbers of the features on your models.

**CAPTION YOUR MAPS:** For each numbered feature on your models and map keys, write a corresponding caption. Each caption should describe a characteristic of the numbered part of the land feature and tell how it was formed or changed by wind or water.

**COMMUNICATE:** Display your models, maps, and captions for the class. Look at the models and maps made by other students. What do all the models and maps have in common? How do some of them differ?

_____

_____

_____

_____

✓ **Checklist**

**Review your project and check off each completed item.**

_____ Includes two 3D models of a land feature

_____ Models the same land feature before and after a change

_____ Includes a topographic map corresponding to each model

_____ Includes captions for at least three details on each model

_____ Captions explain the processes and time involved in the change shown between the two models

# Unit Review

**1.** Which of these can be a positive effect of flooding?
Circle the correct choice.

    **a.** It can enrich farm soil.

    **b.** It can protect roads from erosion.

    **c.** It can keep a river within its banks.

    **d.** It can keep a river from flowing too rapidly.

**2.** Complete the sentences using the words from the
word bank.

> **slow-moving**    **flooding**    **freezing**
>
> **fast-moving**    **erosion**    **deposition**

A glacier is a huge, _____ block, or river, of ice.

Glaciers cause _____ when they are active and

_____ when they melt.

**3.** Indicate whether each phrase describes a desert (*D*),
a rain forest (*R*), or both (*B*) by writing the letter on the
line.

_____ hot climate

_____ low precipitation

_____ high precipitation

_____ large variety of organisms

_____ limited number of organisms

**4.** Complete the sentences using the words from the
word bank.

> **weathering**   **erosion**   **sand**   **dirt**   **water**   **ice**

This photograph shows one common cause of

_____. Another is the freezing and expansion

of _____ during cold weather.

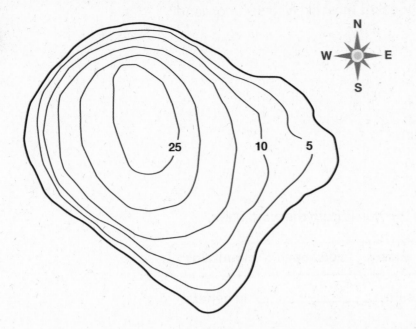

**5.** Use the map to answer the question. Which side of the mountain is the least steep?

   **a.** north

   **b.** south

   **c.** east

   **d.** west

**6.** Which choices name a specific type of map? Circle all that apply.

   **a.** key

   **b.** scale

   **c.** road

   **d.** weather

   **e.** topographic

**7.** Which landforms exist beneath the ocean but not on dry land? Circle the correct choice.

   **a.** volcanoes

   **b.** Ring of Fire

   **c.** trenches

   **d.** mountains

**8.** Where are volcanoes and earthquakes most likely to occur on land? Select all that apply

    **a.** near coasts

    **b.** all over a continent

    **c.** near the Ring of Fire

    **d.** in higher areas like mountains

    **e.** only in the ocean

**9.** Complete the sentences using the words from the word bank.

| earthquakes | continents | oceans | volcanoes | mountains |

Ocean trenches are found beneath _____ . In general,

ocean trenches form on the edges of _____ and oceans.

**10.** Which of the following played a role in the formation of the landscape shown here? Circle all that apply.

    **a.** erosion

    **b.** eruption

    **c.** elevation

    **d.** deposition

    **e.** weathering

# Rocks and Fossils

Explore Online

**Unit Project: DinoZoo**
What kind of zoo habitat would it take to house a dinosaur? You will research a dinosaur's needs and design a zoo space for it with your team. Ask your teacher for details.

© Houghton Mifflin Harcourt • Image Credits: ©Daniel LeClair/Getty Images

Discoveries of fossil remains of extinct animals teach scientists about Earth's environmental past.

# At a Glance

## Vocabulary Game: **Picture It**

**Materials**
- Kitchen timer or online computer timer
- Sketch pad

**Directions**
1. Take turns to play.
2. To take a turn, choose a vocabulary word. Do not tell the word to the other players.
3. Set the timer for one minute.
4. Give clues about the word by drawing pictures on the sketch pad. Draw only pictures and numbers. Do not write words.
5. The first player to guess the word gets 1 point and the next turn. If that player can use the word in a sentence, he or she gets 1 more point.
6. The first player to score 5 points wins.

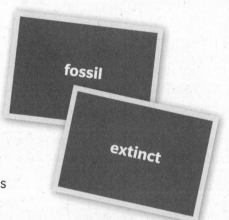

# Unit Vocabulary

**aquatic fossil:** The remains or traces of an organism that lived in water long ago.

**extinct:** Describes a kind of thing that is no longer found on Earth.

**fossil:** The remains or traces of an organism that lived long ago.

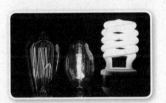

**relative age:** The age of one thing compared to another.

**terrestrial fossil:** The remains or traces of an organism that lived on land long ago.

# How Do Rock Layers Change?

Rocks can give clues about things that happened on Earth long ago. They can also provide evidence of how our planet has changed over time. Some of these rocks formed in ancient oceans. Some of them formed on dry land. What else might rock layers tell us about the past?

## By the end of this lesson . . .
you'll be able to determine the relative age of rock layers and explain how rock layers change.

## Can You Explain It?

Look at the photos. Rock like this can often contain fossils within its layers. Fossils form when ancient living things die and become preserved in rocks. Fossils are found in some types of rocks.

1. The rocks in the photos belong to a group of rocks called the Niobrara chalk formation. How do you think these rocks formed? Which rock layer is the oldest? Which is the youngest?

_____

_____

_____

_____

_____

_____

_____

**Tip**

Learn more about some of Earth's features in How Does Water Shape Earth's Surface? and What Other Factors Shape Earth's Surface?

 **EVIDENCE NOTEBOOK** Look for this icon to help you gather evidence to answer the questions above.

# One Layer at a Time

## Observing Rock Layers

Have you ever seen layers of rocks along a highway or hillside? Have you ever wondered why they look the way they do? This activity will give you some answers to these questions.

**HANDS-ON** Apply What You Know

## Layered Landforms

2. Consider the rock layers you've seen. Different kinds of materials form layers that can become rock. Can you see patterns in rock layers?

Use the materials that your teacher has provided to follow the steps below.

**Step 1:** With your group, select one of the materials. This will be the first layer in your jar.

**Step 2:** Watch as your teacher shows how to pour the material into the jar.

**Step 3:** Pour the material you selected into the jar at a steady rate for 4 seconds.

**Step 4:** Repeat step 3 three times. Change the material and length of time you pour each time. Pour one time for 7 seconds, another time for 13 seconds, and another time for 10 seconds. However, always pour at the same rate.

Which rock layer in your model is the oldest? Which is the youngest? How did pouring the material for different amounts of time affect the layers? What can this tell you about rock layers in nature? What other factors could cause the same thing to happen?

_____

_____

## Layer Upon Layer

These photos show rocks in places from different parts of the world. Yet all the rocks have something in common. Study the photos, and then answer the question.

Explore Online

Akaroa Head is in New Zealand, an island nation not far from Australia. These rock layers have been changed by the ocean and the wind.

The Alps are mountains that stretch across Europe. These mountains are made of many layers of different types of rocks.

Antarctica's Buckley Formation formed almost 300 million years ago! Some of the rocks in this formation include coal, a rock that formed in ancient swamps.

The rock layers surrounding this waterfall are near Stoney Creek, Ontario. The rock layers show many different colors of rock.

**3.** Explain how all the rock layers shown on this page are the same.

_____

_____

_____

# How Some Rocks Form

Many cities across the United States have recycling programs in which used items are collected and used to make new items. Read on to find out how recycling newspapers is similar to the way a series of rock layers can form.

## Layer Over Layer

**4.** On Day 1, a family drops a newspaper into a large recycling bin. The newspaper falls to the bottom of the bin as it's thrown in. On Day 2, another paper is put into the bin. The family drops one newspaper into the bin each day. Label the missing days on the bins below.

 Explore Online

Day 1

_____     _____

**5.** Think about the newspapers in the recycling bin. Which layer is the oldest? youngest? The image below shows the papers on Day 9. Circle the youngest layer and draw an arrow to the oldest layer. Put an X over the layers that are not the oldest or youngest.

Scientists can tell the relative age of rocks by looking at where they fall in a sequence. **Relative age** is the age of one thing compared to another. Relative age explains things in terms of *older* and *younger*. For example, the newspaper from Day 1 is older than the newspaper from Day 3.

**6.** Look at your answers to question 5. How did you know which layer was the oldest? The youngest? Provide evidence to support your answer.

_____

_____

_____

_____

**7. Language SmArts** Research some rock layers near your house or in your state. Find evidence from informational texts to support that the oldest layers of rock are at the bottom of the sequence, and the youngest are at the top.

_____

_____

_____

**EVIDENCE NOTEBOOK** Use what you've learned on these pages to help you explain how the Niobrara chalk may have formed.

## Putting It Together

**8.** Choose the words or phrases that correctly complete each sentence.

| at the top | at the bottom | in the middle |
|---|---|---|
| older | younger | |

In a sequence of rock layers, the oldest layer of rock is

_____ of the sequence. The youngest layer is

_____. As the layers form, _____ rock

forms on top of _____ rock.

# Layer on Layer

## Telling a Story

Mushroom Rock from South Africa, which is shown in the photo below, is made of many layers of rocks. Each rock layer formed in a certain way and gives clues about how this part of Earth changed over time.

### A Long, Long Story!

**9.** Use a thin highlighter or a pen to trace the tops and bottoms of as many layers as you can pick out in this photo of Mushroom Rock. Then number the layers, marking the oldest layer as 1.

 Explore Online

Some of the rocks that make up Mushroom Rock are millions of years old. The layers have been exposed through weathering and erosion.

**10.** How many rock layers did you count?

_____

**11.** What number did you assign to the youngest layer in the rock?

_____

_____

_____

# Do the Math
# Canyon Clues

**12.** You have data about five rock layers labeled A through E. Use these clues to determine the relative ages of the rocks from youngest to oldest, and complete the table.

- Layer A is 200 million years old, but it is 100 million years younger than Layer C.
- Layer B is the top layer of rock.
- Layer C has more layers above it than below it.
- Layer D is older than Layer B and younger than Layer A.
- Layer E is 480 million years old.

| Youngest | |
|---|---|
| 1 | Layer _____ : |
| 2 | Layer _____ : |
| 3 | Layer _____ : |
| 4 | Layer _____ : |
| 5 | Layer _____ : |
| Oldest | |

## Language SmArts
# Conducting Research

**13.** Many of the rock layers in Mushroom Rock are sedimentary rocks. Use informational texts to find out more about sedimentary rocks and how they form. Can you find a relationship between the types of rock and the color of the layers? Write your findings below.

_____

_____

_____

_____

_____

## Some Rocks and Fossils From Around the World

Rock layers are found all over the world. Many of these rocks contain fossils. Fossils provide clues about the ages of the rocks in which they are found. Look at the map and photos and read the captions to learn about some rock formations around the world. Look for patterns in the rocks shown.

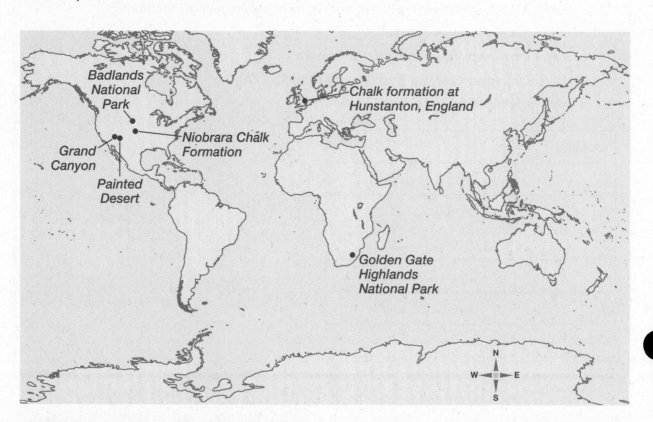

Some rocks in the Grand Canyon, in the southwestern United States, contain many fossils. But there are no dinosaur fossils. Why? The youngest fossils in the rocks are 270 million years old. Dinosaurs lived 230–65 million years ago.

Rocks in the Painted Desert in Arizona contain fossils from a time period spanning millions of years. The oldest fossils are older than dinosaurs, while the youngest are just a few thousand years old.

The Niobrara Chalk in Kansas, Nebraska and other states, is made of millions of fossils of marine algae. This means that Kansas and nearby states were once on the ocean floor!

The Badlands of South Dakota contain young fossils of the close relatives of modern deer, horses, mice, and turtles.

The Ferriby Chalk cliffs in England were part of the ocean floor about 100 million years ago. Fossils of many ocean plants and animals are embedded in this soft rock.

The Mushroom Rock formation in South Africa is home to the oldest fossilized dinosaur egg nest found to date. The nest is 190 million years old!

**14.** Look again at the photos of the rocks and reread the captions to complete the table below.

| Location | Description of rocks/fossils |
|---|---|
| Grand Canyon in SW United States | |
| Painted Desert in Arizona | |
| Niobrara Chalk in Kansas | |
| Badlands of South Dakota | |
| Ferriby Chalk in England | |
| Mushroom Rock in South Africa | |

## Patterns in Rock Layers

You have learned that some rocks are very similar to one another, while other rocks are quite different. Some rocks contain fossils of similar ages. Other rocks contain fossils of different ages.

### Patterns in Layers

**15.** Look again at these photos. Look for patterns from your observations to help you answer the question below.

Grand Canyon

Niobrara Chalk Formation

Ferriby Chalk Formation

**16.** Choose the words or phrases to correctly complete each sentence.

| flat | light | thinner | bent | black | thicker |

These rocks are made of layers that are _____. The layers in

two of the photos are _____ in color. The light layer in the

Ferriby Chalk formation is _____ than the other layers.

 **EVIDENCE NOTEBOOK** The rocks in these photos all contain layers. How do your observations here help you answer the questions from the beginning of this lesson?

## Rocked and Rolled?

Forces and processes on Earth can cause rocks to change. What might happen to rocks when forces act on them?

Explore Online

Some rocks will bend due to temperature and pressure.

Others will break and crack during an earthquake.

17. Look again at the photos above. Compare them with the other photos you've seen so far in this lesson. Use your observations to complete each sentence with the correct word.

In rock layers that have not been disturbed, the _____

rocks are at the bottom and the _____ rocks are at the

top. Due to heat and pressure, some rocks often _____

and an earthquake may _____ rocks.

> youngest
> oldest
> bend
> crack

18. How does finding rock layers made of different types of rock provide evidence that the landscape has changed over time?

_____

_____

## Putting It Together

19. Choose the word that best completes each sentence.

> are layered    were bent by earthquakes    top
> bottom    change    stay the same

Rocks in the Grand Canyon _____. The oldest fossils in

these rocks are found in the _____ layers. Broken rock

layers show that forces have caused a _____ in the layers.

467

© Houghton Mifflin Harcourt • Image Credits: (r) ©Atelopus/istock/Getty Images Plus/Getty Images; (l) ©Matauw/iStock/Getty Images Plus/Getty Images

# Modeling How Rocks Can Form and Change

## Objective

**Collaborate** with a partner to model how rock layers might form and how these layers can change.

What question will you investigate to meet this objective?

_____

_____

_____

**Materials**
- several colors of modeling clay
- paper plate

## Procedure

**STEP 1** Choose one lump of clay. Flatten it into a layer on the paper plate.

What can you say about this model rock layer?

_____

_____

_____

**STEP 2** Choose another color of clay. Flatten it into a layer that sits on top of your first layer.

Why did you choose a different color of clay for this step?

_____

_____

© Houghton Mifflin Harcourt

**STEP 3** Continue placing new layers of clay of different colors on top of each other until you have at least six layers. You may reuse colors as long as layers of the same color don't touch.

Why couldn't model rock layers of the same color touch?

_____

_____

**STEP 4** As you build your model, think about how the model rock layers are like real rock layers. Draw a picture of your finished model in the box below.

**STEP 5** Think about ways you can change your model to show how forces can change rock layers. Make the model look like one of the photos in this lesson. Explain how you will change it on the lines below.

_____

_____

_____

**STEP 6** Share your results with other students. Discuss ways other types of changes can be represented. Then change your model. On a separate piece of paper, draw pictures of your before and after model. Label the drawings, and submit the paper to your teacher.

## Analyze Your Results

**STEP 7**  Compare and contrast the layers before and after you changed them.

_____

_____

_____

**STEP 8**  Did the order of the layers in your model change when you changed the model?

_____

_____

_____

**STEP 9**  Which rock layer in your model is the oldest? Which is the youngest?

_____

_____

_____

## Draw Conclusions

**STEP 10**  Make a claim about rock layers.

_____

_____

_____

**STEP 11**  Cite evidence to support your claim.

_____

_____

_____

**STEP 12**  Write at least two more questions you would like to ask about how rock layers form and change.

_____

_____

_____

# Not What It Used to Be

## It's a *Grand* Canyon!

The layers of rock that make up the Grand Canyon formed over millions and millions of years.

 Explore Online

 **HANDS-ON  Apply What You Know**

### The Story of the Canyon

Look at these images of the Grand Canyon.

Dozens of rock layers can be seen in the Grand Canyon.

The Colorado River flows through the Grand Canyon.

20. Put on your creative cap! You're going to be a cartoonist! Draw a cartoon strip that shows how you think the Grand Canyon formed. Your strip should have at least three panels (boxes). Be sure to show what the land looked like before, during, and after formation of the canyon. Submit your cartoon to your teacher.

Once the layers were in place, the mighty Colorado River began to carve through them to create the long, deep canyon we see today.

21. In your own words, briefly explain how the Grand Canyon formed.

_____

_____

_____

# Slow and Steady

Rivers are narrow bodies of water that flow over land. They can change the rocks beneath them by carving canyons. Look at the images and read the captions to find out how.

**Explore Online**

**1.** As a river flows over flat land, it slowly cuts down into the rocks.

**2.** Over time, the river cuts deeper and deeper into the rocks, making the riverbed's walls steeper.

**3.** After millions of years, a deep canyon with very steep walls can form.

**22.** How does a canyon such as the Grand Canyon form? Circle the best answer.

    **a.** Earthquakes cause rocks to break and form a canyon.

    **b.** Rock layers are put down in two places to form a canyon.

    **c.** A river carves down into rocks to form a deep canyon.

    **d.** Rain and snow cause rocks to dissolve to form a canyon.

You've just learned one way changes to a landscape can occur slowly over time. Other forces on Earth can change the land quickly. Look at the image on the next page to find out more.

# In the Blink of an Eye!

Earthquakes can change the landscape very quickly. In fact, most earthquakes last for less than a minute! Look at the drawings to see what happens to rocks during these events.

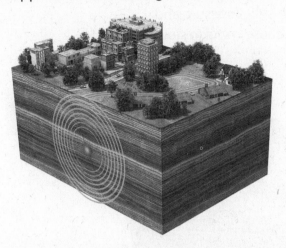

Over time, stored energy builds up in rocks.

During an earthquake, rocks move and the stored energy is released.

Earthquakes happen in many places around the world. But most, about 75%, occur along the edges of the Pacific Ocean. This active area is called the Ring of Fire. Many volcanoes are located there, too.

### Engineer It!
# Measuring Earthquakes

**23.** Scientists use seismometers to detect and measure the energy released by earthquakes. The top image shows an early seismometer. The needle records the earthquake activity on the paper. The bottom photo shows a modern seismometer that uses digital technology to record the earthquake activity. What advantages might the modern way or recording data have over older ones?

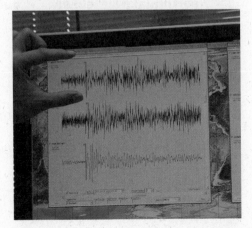

_____

_____

_____

_____

# What Else Can Change Rock Layers?

You've learned that rivers can slowly carve rock layers into deep canyons. You've also learned that earthquakes can cause rocks to quickly break. What other things can change the landscape? The layers of rocks in the drawing are under a lot of pressure from each side. Pressure and high temperatures deep below Earth's surface can cause rocks to slowly bend and change.

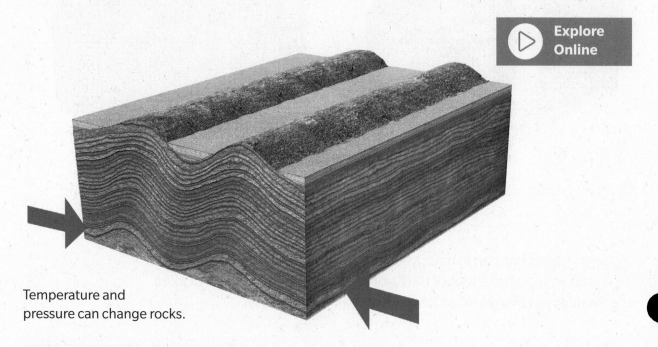

Temperature and pressure can change rocks.

**24.** Describe in your own words what is happening to the rock above.

_____

_____

**25.** Choose the words or phrases to correctly complete each sentence.

| bend | break | river |
|---|---|---|
| earthquake | slowly | quickly |

The Grand Canyon formed as a(n) _____ eroded rock

layers. The changes happened _____. Earthquakes change

the land also. They can cause rocks to _____.

High temperatures and pressures deep within Earth often cause rocks

to _____.

What are some other ways that processes and forces can change the landscape? Look at the images and read the captions to find out.

Rock layers can be changed by wind, water, and gravity. Natural bridges, such as this one, form when wind and water break rock into smaller pieces. Gravity causes the loose materials to fall to the ground. Eventually, an arch is carved into the rocks.

Glaciers are very large masses of ice and snow. Rocks frozen into the sides and bottoms of glaciers can carve deep grooves into the land as the ice slides over it. As a glacier slowly flows across the ground, rock layers can be weathered and eroded to form a canyon.

26. Explain two ways in which a glacier can change rock layers.

_____

_____

_____

 **EVIDENCE NOTEBOOK** Consider what you've learned about how landscapes change over time. Write your thoughts in your notebook.

## Patterns as Evidence

**27.** Many rocks form horizontal layers. But these layers can change over time. Use what you've learned to match each image to what changed the rocks.

pressure

glacier

river

wind

water

gravity

temperature

**28.** Choose the word or phrase that best completes each sentence.

Changes to _____ can be slow or fast.

_____ can slowly carve canyons into the land.

_____ can carve deep grooves into rocks.

Rocks deep within Earth can be bent by _____.

_____ can cause rocks to break.

| rock layers | rivers |
|---|---|
| earthquakes | glaciers |
| pressure and temperature | |

### Language SmArts
## Citing Evidence

**29.** Many times, you can't see the processes that change rock layers. So what evidence do you have that a landscape has been changed?

_____

_____

_____

_____

_____

**Tip**

The English Language Arts Handbook can provide help with understanding how to cite evidence.

# Discover More

**Check out this path . . . or go online to choose one of these other paths.**

**People in Science & Engineering**

- **Rock Diversity**
- **Why It's Grand**

## People in Science and Engineering

### Bernard Hubbard

Bernard Hubbard was a geologist and explorer who led expeditions in Alaska from the late 1920s to the early 1960s. Not only did he explore glaciers and volcanoes as a scientist, he led expeditions for other people so they could see the geologic wonders in Alaska's remote wilderness, too.

▶ Explore Online

Hubbard explored lakes in volcanic craters and other features that are very difficult to reach. He documented many geological features in Alaska with photographs.

Bernard Hubbard was a good writer and a skilled filmmaker in his time. He gave frequent public lectures, and he was an early producer of science and nature media programs before such programs were common. His photographs provide a record of the landscape around glaciers that today's scientists can look at to see how the glaciers have changed.

**30.** Imagine you are going to interview Bernard Hubbard. What questions would you ask? What answers would you expect him to give? Create a mock interview on the lines below. Write your questions and Mr. Hubbard's possible responses.

_____

_____

_____

_____

# Moraines

A moraine is a landform or feature of sand, gravel, and rock that has been deposited by a glacier. Moraines can have features called kettles, which are dips that form when a large chunk of ice inside the debris pile melts and the surface of the moraine collapses into the hole.

As glaciers move, they weather rock. Some weathered pieces of rock become stuck in the ice. The rock is deposited as the glaciers move and melt.

Glaciers form moraines in these ways. The ridges that form to the sides of the glacier's path are called *lateral moraines*. A pile of debris that forms at the advancing end of a glacier is called a *terminal moraine*.

**31.** Diagram a glacier producing two lateral moraines and a terminal moraine in a wide valley.

Label the parts of your diagram. Write captions that tell which of the moraines is the oldest formation and why.

# Lesson Check

Name _____

## Can You Explain It?

1. Remember the Niobrara Chalk formation from the beginning of the lesson? Where do you think its rock layers came from? Which layer is the oldest? Explain your thinking below. Be sure to do the following:

Explore Online

- Describe how the rocks might have formed.

- Explain what you can conclude about their relative age.

- Identify the oldest and youngest layers.

**EVIDENCE NOTEBOOK** Use the information you've collected in your Evidence Notebook to help you cover each point above.

_____

_____

_____

_____

_____

_____

_____

_____

## Checkpoints

2. Which of the following are examples of slow changes to rock layers?
   a. A river cuts a canyon into rock.
   b. Rocks are broken by an earthquake.
   c. Glaciers carve a valley into the rock.
   d. Pressure from above presses sediment into rock.

**3.** In undisturbed rock layers, the youngest layer is always _____.

  **a.** on top

  **b.** on the bottom

  **c.** the thinnest

  **d.** the thickest

**4.** Your family is riding in a car. You see some rock layers in a hillside. Your little sister asks how the rocks got there. How can you best explain it to her? Circle the best answer.

  **a.** Tell her how earthquakes are measured.

  **b.** Remind her how your family puts newspapers into a recycling bin every day.

  **c.** Tell her about the Grand Canyon.

  **d.** Remind her how sand at the playground can be shaped into layers.

**5.** Use the words in the bank to complete the sentences.

> earthquakes    fossils    glaciers    rivers

_____ and _____ can change rocks slowly while

_____ can change rock layers quickly.

**6.** Use the words in the bank to complete the sentences.

> are layered    similar    different
>
> were bent by earthquakes    change    stay the same

Rocks in the Grand Canyon _____. Rock layers around the

world exhibit _____ patterns. All of the rocks in the canyon

will _____ over time.

# Lesson Roundup

**A.** Which of these is true of rock layers? Circle all that apply.

   **a.** They are always flat.

   **b.** They can be different ages.

   **c.** They can only change during earthquakes.

   **d.** They can change slowly or quickly.

   **e.** They can bend or break.

   **f.** They all contain the same type of rock.

......................................................................................

**B.** On each line, write the word or phrase that best completes each sentence.

| at the top | Colorado River | slowly | near the bottom |

The Grand Canyon is a landform in the southwestern United States. It

formed as the _____ flowed over rock layers. The oldest

rocks in the canyon are _____. The youngest rocks are

_____. The canyon formed very _____.

......................................................................................

**C.** Explain how pressure, temperature, wind, water, and gravity can change rocks.

_____

_____

_____

_____

_____

_____

_____

_____

_____

# What Do Fossils Tell Us About Ancient Environments?

Fossils are the remains of ancient life that have been preserved over time. They can tell us much about how plants and animals of the past lived and died. They can also tell us about the environments in which those plants and animals lived.

**By the end of this lesson . . .**

you'll be able to make inferences about ancient environments and organisms from fossil evidence.

# Can You Explain It?

Explore
Online

This is Petrified Forest National Park. Imagine what it feels like to walk through the area. You can almost feel the heat and dryness of the desert just by looking at the photos.

**1.** Think about the type of environment this used to be. Was it like the present-day environment of the Petrified Forest? What can you infer about this area millions of years ago from the presence of fossil trees?

**Tip**

Learn more about rock layers in *How Do Rock Layers Change?*

_____

_____

_____

_____

_____

_____

**EVIDENCE NOTEBOOK** Look for this icon to help you gather evidence to answer the questions above.

# Clues from the Past

## Check It Out!

Earth is billions of years old. Many types of plants and animals have lived on Earth during that time. But many of them, like the dinosaurs, died out long ago.

Even though dinosaurs aren't around now, we know they were once here. How? We can look at fossils. A **fossil** is the remains or traces of an organism that lived long ago.

Take a look at the fossil below. It is the fossil of a reptile that lived at the same time as the dinosaurs but is now extinct. **Extinct** organisms are no longer found on Earth. Think about the types of things you can learn by looking at the fossil.

**Explore Online**

**Plesiosaur fossil**

2. In the space below, record two observations about the fossil. What can you infer about the fossil from your observations?

_____

_____

_____

_____

_____

_____

_____

**3.** Circle all the statements about the fossil that are true. Go back and observe the fossil again if you cannot recall what you saw.

 **a.** This is a fossil of an animal.

 **b.** This organism had a long neck.

 **c.** This organism had a large, round head.

 **d.** The fossil bones show legs that look like flippers.

 **e.** This creature had no tail.

 **EVIDENCE NOTEBOOK** Take a look at the plesiosaur fossil. In your Evidence Notebook, write down all of the features that you can identify from the fossil. Infer what these features might have been used for.

 **Language SmArts**
# Compare and Contrast

**Tip**

The English Language Arts Handbook can provide help with understanding how to compare and contrast.

**4.** Think about the body shape of the plesiosaur. Compare it to something else that looks similar. It could be a vehicle or other object, or it could be a living thing. In the box below, draw the object you are comparing to the fossil. Circle similar structures in your drawing and the fossil on the previous page. Explain your comparison in the table that follows.

| Fossil | |
|---|---|
| | |

**HANDS-ON ACTIVITY**

# Old and New

## Objective

**Collaborate** with others in your group to identify the structures and features of fossils. You can then determine how and where the fossil lived.

What question will you investigate to meet this objective?

_____

_____

**Materials**
- fossil kit
- magnifying glass
- classification chart

**STEP 1** With your group, place all the fossils from your fossil kit on a table in front of you. What do all the fossils have in common?

_____

_____

_____

_____

**STEP 2** Observe each fossil one by one with the magnifying glass. Use your senses of sight and touch to determine the characteristics of each one. Why is using your sense of touch important?

_____

_____

**STEP 3** Record your observations and conclusions about each fossil in the table at the top of the next page. Share your results with the class.

© Houghton Mifflin Harcourt

486

| Fossil | What evidence tells us how this organism lived? | Did the organism live on land or in water? | What are some similar living things today? |
| --- | --- | --- | --- |
| | | | |
| | | | |
| | | | |
| | | | |
| | | | |
| | | | |

## Analyze Your Results

**STEP 4** What evidence did you use to determine whether an organism lived on land or in water?

_____

_____

**STEP 5** Based on the data you collected, how many organisms lived on land and how many lived in water?

_____

## Draw Conclusions

**STEP 6** Make a claim about the relationship between fossil animals and animals living today. Cite evidence to support your claim

_____

_____

**STEP 7** What is one question you have about fossils?

_____

_____

# Then and Now

## Seeing the Past

We can use the structures of an organism's body to tell where it lived. But how similar to today's organisms are animals that lived millions of years ago?

The pairs of pictures below show fossils and illustrations of what the real organisms may have looked like. Observe each pair closely.

Explore Online

The fossil is of a plant called a fern. Ferns are ancient plants that were around hundreds of millions of years ago. There are many types of ferns today, too, but most of them grow in places that are warm and moist. It is easy to spot the delicate leaves, or fronds, of a fern plant.

The fossil skeleton is of an Irish elk. The Irish elk was the largest of an extinct type of deer that lived in Europe and Asia about 2.5 million years ago. You can see the elk's slender legs and massive antlers—up to 4 meters (13 feet) from tip to tip!

The fossil skeleton is of a mosasaur. The mosasaurs are an extinct group of reptiles. They had long, narrow bodies and long snouts. The mososaurs had short, flattened limbs that looked like paddles.

**5.** Complete each sentence using the best word or phrase from the bank.

| land | underground | in the water | antlers | legs | flippers |
|------|-------------|--------------|---------|------|----------|
| the forest | water | the air | | | |

Most plants, such as ferns, live on _____. Deer and their

relatives, such as the Irish elk, use their slender _____ to walk

through forests and meadows. The paddle-like limbs of the mosasaur helped it

move through _____.

 **Language SmArts**
# Comparing Structures

**6.** Research two methods scientists use to learn about fossils. Write how each method helps scientists understand the environment the fossil came from.

_____

_____

_____

 **EVIDENCE NOTEBOOK** In your Evidence Notebook, list the parts of the organisms that give clues to the environment where the organisms lived. Then identify the type of environment where organisms with those parts did live.

# Cousins?

Sometimes fossils can be the ancestors of modern-day organisms, or they can be similar-looking organisms.

## Matching Fossils and Organisms

**7.** Draw a line from the image of the fossil in the first column to the image of the modern organism it most closely resembles in the second column.

**8.** What features helped you match them up?

_____

_____

_____

_____

_____

_____

# Past Meets Present

9. Look at the image in the amber fossil and describe what you see.

   You have learned that fossils can give clues about the environment in which the organism lived. Apply what you have learned.

   Research two fossils. For each fossil, find a related or similar modern-day organism and determine what type of environment it lives in. Infer whether the organisms that became fossils lived in similar environments.

## Putting It Together

10. Read the paragraph. Choose the correct words to complete each sentence. Write the words on the lines.

| photographs | fossils | skeletons |
|---|---|---|
| remains | bones | shapes |
| animals | related | infer |
| the same | different | |

We learn about the organisms of long ago from _____.

They are the _____, or traces, of organisms that lived in

the past. Many animals alive today have structures that are similar to

_____ that lived in the past. The similarities suggest that the

organisms are _____. When we study today's organisms, we can

_____ things about related organisms of the past.

# Ancient Lands

## Fossils and Environments

We can learn a lot from fossils. Many times fossils can indicate the type of environment where the organism lived. Organisms that lived in water leave behind **aquatic fossils**. **Terrestrial fossils** are left behind by organisms that lived on land. The features of the fossil determine which type it is.

### Fossils and Ancient Lands

**11.** Read the information about each organism and answer whether the fossil is an aquatic fossil or a terrrestrial fossil.

Explore Online

**Ammonites** were animals that lived in coiled shells. They moved by squirting jets of water from their bodies.

_____

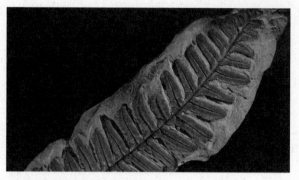

**Ferns** are plants that live in warm, moist environments such as rain forests. This fossil is an imprint of a fern leaf.

_____

**Fish** use their fins and tails to move. They often move in large groups, called schools.

_____

**Snails** are small animals with coiled shells. They slide slowly along surfaces with one flat foot made of muscle.

_____

**Clams** are soft animals that live inside shells. Clams have lived on Earth for millions of years.

**Ants** have jointed body segments and six legs. This one was found inside a bubble of hardened amber.

© Houghton Mifflin Harcourt • Image Credits: (cr) ©jaminwell/istock / getty Images Plus/ Getty Images; (bl) ©Pixtal/Superstock; (tl) ©ElementalImaging/istock / getty Images Plus/ Getty Images; (cl) ©jrroman/Getty Images

 **Do the Math**

## Clues in Footprints

**12.** Dinosaurs that left behind three-toed footprints such as those shown in the photo include *Tyrannosaurus* and *Allosaurus*. At one time, scientists thought these dinosaurs walked upright with their tails dragging behind them and their heads high in the air. Today, we know that their upper bodies leaned forward and were balanced by their tails, which hovered over the ground. Their height is usually measured at their hips.

Did you know that scientists have a way of measuring a dinosaur's hip height? They do it by measuring the dinosaur's footprints. Hip height is four times the length of the footprint. The formula can be expressed this way: $H = 4l$

If a dinosaur's footprint is 35 cm in length, how tall would the dinosaur have been at the hip? Show your calculations.

 **EVIDENCE NOTEBOOK** In your Evidence Notebook, compare the fossils you just saw to the fossils you observed at the start of the lesson. Which are most like those you observed at the beginning? What clues does this provide to where the fossils at the beginning lived? Record your ideas in your Evidence Notebook.

## Identify Your Evidence

Fossils are evidence of past organisms and past environments. On the last page, you identified fossils by their environment. Complete the section below to identify the evidence you used to determine where each fossil belonged.

**13.** Complete the paragraph by writing the correct words to complete each sentence.

| | | | | | |
|---|---|---|---|---|---|
| leaves | arms | tentacles | shell | legs | ammonite |
| fish | dragonfly | clam | fern | walking stick | |

The _____ of the fern fossil are evidence that it was a plant,

and most plants live on land. The _____ of the snail helps

identify it. Some snails live on land. The shells of the _____ and

_____ helped identify them as aquatic animals.

**Language SmArts**

# Compare and Contrast

**14.** Describe how you would determine where an organism lived by analyzing its fossil remains. What features would you look for? Think about the shapes of features and their sizes relative to the rest of the organism. Recall information from your experiences in this lesson as you develop your response.

_____

_____

_____

_____

_____

_____

_____

_____

_____

_____

**Tip**

The English Language Arts Handbook can provide help with understanding how to compare and contrast.

# Discover More

**Check out this path . . . or go online to choose one of these other paths.**

| Where Are They? | • Fossil Hangouts
• How Do They Compare |

## Where Are They?

Take a look at the three fossils. Research each one, and identify four different places where each fossil has been found. Describe the current environment in these locations as well.

Ammonites were squid-like sea animals with coiled shells. They died out 65 million years ago, at the same time as the dinosaurs.

Polyps live inside a limestone skeleton that remains after they die and is called coral. The oldest coral fossils date back 500 million years.

The earliest jawed fishes appeared about 416 million years ago. They lived in many parts of ancient seas.

495

**15.** On the map below, mark an *X* for the places where ammonite fossils have been found. Use a dot for coral. Mark a triangle for the locations of the jawed fishes.

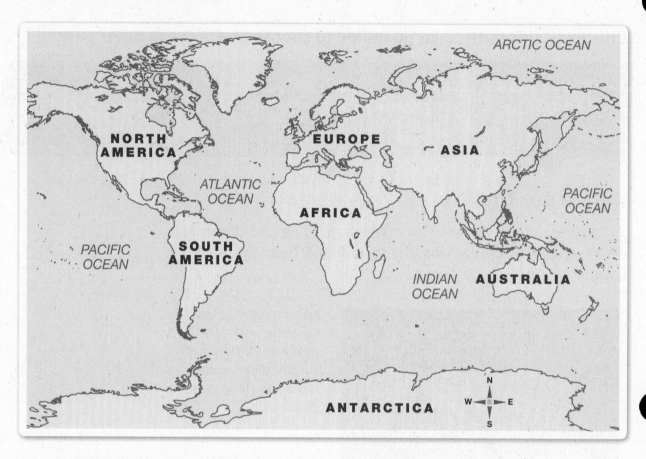

**16.** The three fossils were found on land. Consider the types of animals whose remains became the fossils. Were the areas where the fossils were found the same types of environments when the animals were alive? Include an explanation for your answer.

_____

_____

_____

**17.** What conclusions can you draw about the fact that aquatic fossils are often found in areas that are far away from today's seas? Circle all that apply.

   **a.** Earth's surface was different long ago.

   **b.** The world did not have land when fossils formed.

   **c.** Some places that are dry land now were once covered by water.

   **d.** Fossils never form on dry land.

# Lesson Check

Name _____

## Can You Explain It?

Explore Online

1. Think back to the fossil you saw at the beginning of the lesson. Explain what we can learn from the fossil. Be sure to do the following:

• Explain how the fossil represents the original organism.

• Identify similar structures found in organisms today.

• Describe how the type of fossil and structures show where it lived.

 **EVIDENCE NOTEBOOK** Use the information you've collected in your Evidence Notebook to help you cover each point above.

_____
_____
_____
_____
_____
_____
_____
_____
_____
_____

## Checkpoints

2. What do some fossils and modern-day organisms have in common? Circle all that apply.

a. They are the same age.

b. They may be related.

c. They may have similar body structures.

d. They all come from rock layers.

3. Which statement is true about fossils?
   a. Fossils can tell us what animals looked like millions of years ago.
   b. Fossils are never organisms that lived in the sea.
   c. Fossils found today are always terrestrial fossils.
   d. Fossils can tell us how animals become extinct.

4. Which of the following would be evidence of the kind of environment a fossilized organism lived in? Circle all that apply.
   a. flat, paddle-like limbs and a broad tail with two fins
   b. jointed legs
   c. a long tail
   d. a small head

5. You are digging in a desert in the mountains and find fossil imprints of ferns. Based on this, which type of environment did the mountain used to be?
   a. a warmer and drier environment
   b. a colder and drier environment
   c. a warmer and moister environment
   d. a deep, watery environment

6. Write *aquatic* or *terrestrial* on each line to tell which type of environment the organism lived in.

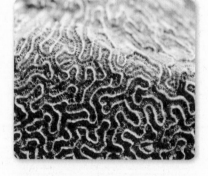

_____

_____

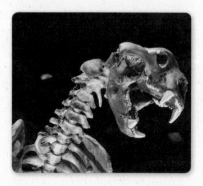

_____

_____

# Lesson Roundup

**A.** Choose the answer that best completes each sentence.

| they died    they grew    they lived |

Observing the structures of fossils allows scientists to make inferences

about the way _____ .

| the same as    similar to    nothing like |

Fossils show us that many organisms alive today, such as

corals, are _____ organisms that lived millions of years ago.

| lake    desert    swamp |

The discovery of a fossil fern leaf means that the environment in that area

was most likely a _____ millions of years ago.

........................................................................................

**B.** You see a fossil with a long, narrow skeleton. It has four limbs that
look like flippers. What can you infer about the kind of animal this
was and where it lived?

_____

_____

........................................................................................

**C.** Scientists find a fossil that is millions of years old. Its body structure
is similar to animals that are alive today. What can the scientist infer
about the ancient animal and today's animal?

_____

_____

........................................................................................

**D.** Why are fossils important in understanding Earth's past?

_____

_____

# What Are Some Patterns Fossils Show Us?

Today, these mangrove trees grow near a watery environment. Do you think this environment has always looked like this?

_____

## By the end of this lesson . . .
you'll be able to use information from fossils and rock layers to describe how an environment has changed over time and determine the relative ages of those fossils and rock layers.

# Can You Explain It?

Scientists found this fossilized sea turtle in a desert. Like sea turtles today, ancient sea turtles moved by using powerful flippers to swim through the water. Their bony shells offered some protection against large predators.

**1.** How did this fossilized sea turtle end up in the desert? What can fossils like this tell us about the past?

_____

_____

_____

_____

_____

_____

**Tip**

Learn more about rock layers and fossils in How Do Rock Layers Change? and What Do Fossils Tell Us About Ancient Environments?

 **EVIDENCE NOTEBOOK** Look for this icon to help you gather evidence to answer the questions above.

# HANDS-ON ACTIVITY
# Layer By Layer

## Objective

**Collaborate** with your group to investigate how to use evidence to determine what an environment was like.

What question will you investigate to meet this objective?

_____

_____

### Materials
- nature magazines
- colored pencils
- scissors
- circular stencils
- construction paper
- white construction paper for drawing
- tape

## Procedure

**STEP 1**  Your teacher will provide you with magazines or other sources of images of present-day environments. Individually, each person in your group will choose a specific environment, such as a desert, swamp, or underwater environment. From the materials provided, select an image that best represents your environment. It should show animals and plants that live there.

**STEP 2**  Use a stencil to cut out two to three round holes in a sheet of construction paper. The round holes will be windows that show some but not all of the organisms in your environment. After cutting the holes, place the construction paper over your drawing paper. Trace the cut out circles on your drawing paper.

What do you think you are modeling by using paper to block portions of the images?

_____

_____

**STEP 3**  Draw or cut out a picture of the environment and its plants and animals. Be sure one plant or animal is in each circle you drew in step 2.

What do you think the climate is like in the environment you chose?

_____

_____

**STEP 4** Place the construction papers on top of your environment. Make sure you can see plants and animals through the windows. Tape the pages together.

**STEP 5** With your group, layer all the environments by stacking them one on top of the other.

What are you modeling when you layer the different pictures on top of each other? What does the stack represent?

_____

_____

**STEP 6** Trade your layers with another group.

**STEP 7** Look at each layer of your new stack. Use the images you can see through the windows of each layer to identify each environment.

**STEP 8** Talk with other members of your group about which environment came first and which came later.

List the environments in the chart, layer by layer, from oldest to youngest. Include observations that helped you identify the environments.

| Relative Age | Observations | Type of Environment |
|---|---|---|
| 1st environment | | |
| 2nd environment | | |
| 3rd environment | | |
| 4th environment | | |
| 5th environment | | |

## Analyze Your Results

**STEP 9** By covering up most of the picture and leaving only a small window to see what lived in that environment, what do you think you modeled?

_____

_____

_____

**STEP 10** Compare your results with those from another group? How are they similar and different?

_____

_____

_____

## Draw Your Conclusion

**STEP 11** Based on where each layer is in the stack, which environment came first in this area? Which is the newest environment?

_____

_____

_____

**STEP 12** Make a claim about fossils and environments, and cite evidence to support it.

| Claim | Evidence |
|-------|----------|
|       |          |
|       |          |
|       |          |
|       |          |

**STEP 13** What is one question you have about fossils and environments?

_____

_____

# Evidence of Environments

## Seeing History

Many locations around the world are rich with fossils. Some of these places have rock layers where fossils from many types of organisms can be found. The fossils below were all found in one of these locations.

### Identify the Fossil

**2.** Look at the fossils. Match each description to the correct fossil.

 **Explore Online**

**a.** This fossil is a snake. You can see its backbone, skull, and ribs.

**b.** Small fossil shrimp are common in this area. This is one example.

**c.** The leaf of a plant clearly shows in this fossil. It is the leaf of a willow tree. Plants give scientists important clues to past environments.

**d.** Some rock layers here are full of fish fossils. Consider the types of environment where fish were common.

# Building the Story

Take a look at the picture. It shows several rock layers.

**3.** Analyze the picture to describe the fossils in the rock layers and the types of environments they would have lived in.

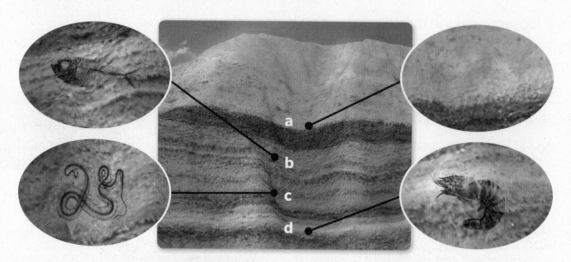

|  | **Type of Fossil** | **Where Organism Lived** |
|---|---|---|
| **Layer A** | leaf | |
| **Layer B** | fish | |
| **Layer C** | snake | |
| **Layer D** | shrimp | |

Choose the correct answer for each question.

**4.** Which rock layer is the oldest?
- **a.** Layer A
- **b.** Layer B
- **c.** Layer C
- **d.** Layer D

**5.** How do you know the layer you chose is the oldest?
- **a.** The oldest layer is usually on top.
- **b.** The oldest layer usually has land animals.
- **c.** The oldest layer is usually on the bottom.
- **d.** The oldest layer is between layers of limestone.

**6.** Use the evidence to identify the oldest type of environment represented in these rock layers.
- **a.** desert
- **b.** sea
- **c.** forest
- **d.** mountain

**EVIDENCE NOTEBOOK** Make a statement about the type of environment one rock layer indicates. Use evidence to support your statement. Record any ideas you may have about how the sea turtle fossil shown at the beginning of the lesson ended up in a desert.

**7.** Look at the four environments below and read their descriptions. Use the rock layers on the previous page as evidence to number the environments in order of age, with 1 being the oldest.

This area was once covered by a freshwater lake. Many fish, turtles, and other aquatic animals lived here at that time. Terrestrial animals also lived on the land around the lake. They used the lake as a drinking source.

Willow trees once grew here. During this time, the climate was much warmer than it is today. It had a temperate to sub-tropical environment, unlike today. Summers were hot and humid, and winters were mild but sometimes cool. Some trees lost their leaves in the winter.

The area was also once covered by a saltwater sea. Many saltwater animals lived in the water including clams, shrimp, sharks and other fish.

At another time, the area was covered by a cypress forest. The ground was moist. Once in awhile, organisms might become trapped in the mud in this environment.

# Global Stories

The types of fossils found in any given location, may also be found in other parts of the world. And the order in which fossils are found in rock layers is often the same at different locations around the globe.

**HANDS-ON** Apply What You Know

## Where Else?

8. Choose a fossil from this lesson that interests you. Research to find out where else in the world it has been found. List those places on a sheet of paper. Use a world map and colored pencils to mark where similar fossils have been found.

9. **Language SmArts** You now have some idea of the types of environments that were available to organisms millions of years ago. What can you infer about how Earth's surface has changed?

_____

_____

## Putting It Together

10. How can fossils serve as evidence of specific events and environments in Earth's history? How can they show patterns in that history?

_____

_____

_____

11. Choose the correct words to complete the sentences.

| shrimp | aquatic | plants |

The rock layers from the previous pages show change over time. The first animals

there were _____. This shows that the environment at the time was

_____. Over time, most of the water disappeared. A forest formed.

The forest had many types of _____ that are common in warm climates.

# More Changes

## Consistent Patterns

The pattern in which rock layers are laid down and evidence of how environments and organisms are preserved can be affected by events at Earth's surface.

**HANDS-ON  Apply What You Know**

### Disordered Days

**12.** You have seen rock layers that lay flat, one on top of the other. But some rock layers are not quite so neat.

   **a.** Label five pieces of paper with the days of the week, starting with Monday.

   **b.** Stack the papers one on top of the other in the order of the days, with Monday at the bottom.

   **c.** Before putting Thursday on the pile, remove Wednesday. Then put Thursday on top of Tuesday.

   **d.** Finish by adding Friday.

   **e.** Create a second set of layers by repeating the first two steps. Do not remove the Wednesday layer this time.

Compare and contrast the two sets of layers. Think about what the missing layer could represent if the layers were made of rock. What could cause a layer to be missing? Answer the questions below.

**13.** Circle the correct answer. How does the first stack model erosion?

   **a.** It has several layers.       **c.** One layer was broken.

   **b.** One layer was removed.    **d.** The layers are all rock.

**14.** Circle the correct answer. Which layer(s) can be eroded?

   **a.** the top layer           **c.** one of the middle layers

   **b.** the bottom layer      **d.** both the top and bottom layers

**15.** Circle the correct answer. What would happen if erosion removed the third layer before the fourth layer formed?

   **a.** The third layer would form again.

   **b.** The second layer would be larger.

   **c.** The fourth layer would be on top of the second.

   **d.** There would be two third layers.

# When Things Change

Look at the rock layers below. Notice that some of the layers have fossils in them.

This column of rock has five layers. Three of the layers contain fossils.

**16.** Using the rock layer image above as a reference, assign layer numbers to the area of rock that was offset by the earthquake. The older layer should be labeled *1*, the youngest *5*.

**17.** What did the earthquake do to the order of the rock layers? Circle the best answer.

    **a.** It did not change the order of the layers.

    **b.** It reversed the order of layers.

    **c.** It removed several of the layers.

    **d.** It created one new layer.

**18.** Sometimes, layers of rock break down through weathering and erosion. Think back to the activity you did on page 509. Then look at the rock layers below. Suppose these layers are part of the same rock layers as the those on the previous page, but at a different location. Again, label each layer, starting with *1* for the oldest layer.

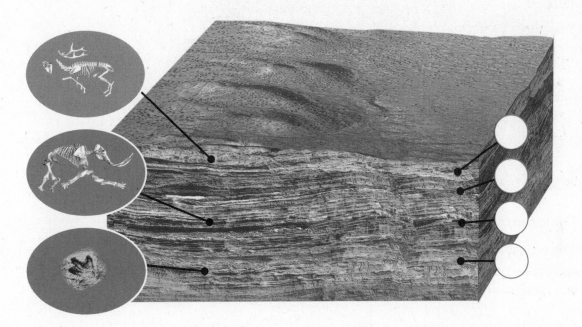

**19.** Compare your numbering here to your numbering in question 16. Is each layer given the same number in both images? Why or why not?

**Language SmArts** Answer the questions below. Circle all that apply.

**20.** What evidence did you use to number the layers?

   **a.** the color of each rock layer

   **b.** the fossils in each rock layer

   **c.** the fact that layers get older as you move down from the surface

   **d.** the fact that an earthquake occurred

   **e.** the fact that erosion occurred

**21.** How do the rock layers show changes in the land over time?

   **a.** They have the same number of layers.

   **b.** The type of fossils found in them change from aquatic to terrestrial.

   **c.** The type of fossils found in them were all aquatic.

   **d.** There are fossils in almost every layer.

   **e.** Disruption to the layers shows change over time.

# Interpret Layers

Use what you've learned about rock layers to answer the questions.

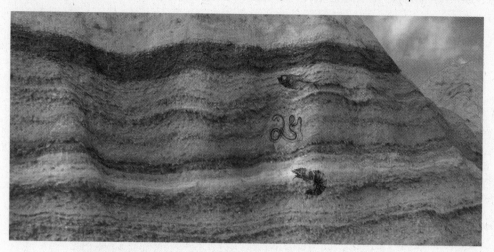

**22.** Circle the correct answer.

The oldest fossil is the fossil shrimp.
**a.** I agree because the shrimp fossil is in the oldest layer.
**b.** I disagree because the leaf fossil is in the oldest layer.

**23.** Circle the correct answer.

The snake lived after the leaf but before the shrimp.
**a.** I agree because the snake fossil is in a younger rock layer than the leaf fossil, but in an older layer than the shrimp fossil.
**b.** I disagree because the snake fossil is in an older rock layer than the leaf fossil and in a younger layer than the shrimp fossil.

 **EVIDENCE NOTEBOOK** How did you determine which layers were oldest and which were youngest? What evidence did you use? How does analyzing rock layers like these help explain why a sea turtle fossil might be found in a desert?

 **Language SmArts**
## Refer Explicitly to Text

**24.** How could fossils in the rock layers help you determine their age if the layers were moved out of their original order?

_____

_____

_____

**Tip**

The English Language Arts Handbook can provide help with understanding how to refer explicitly to text.

# Discover More

**Check out this path . . . or go online to choose one of these other paths.**

| People in Science & Engineering | • Changes in Environments<br>• Careers in Science |
|---|---|

## People in Science and Engineering

### Studying Evidence from the Past

Read these profiles of important people in science. The field of paleontology has changed over time.

Explore Online

**Edward Cope** was a paleontologist who lived in the 1800s. He discovered the fossils of 1,000 species of extinct animals. Many of his discoveries were made during the 1860s. At that time, there was little technology to assist in locating fossils and recovering them.

**Mary Higby Schweitzer** is a modern paleontologist who studies the hidden interiors of fossilized bones. By breaking parts of some specimens down and examining their material under a microscope, she has made new discoveries about dinosaur tissues.

In 1980, **Luis Alvarez,** along with his son, **Walter** proposed a new explanation for the extinction of the dinosaurs. They claimed an asteroid hit Earth 65 million years ago. It threw up dust that blocked the sun for months and caused massive wildfires. The result was the extinction of many species, including the non-avian dinosaurs.

**Patricia Vickers-Rich** is a paleontologist. She studies the fossils of animals that lived in Australia and, with her husband, has discovered several new species of dinosaur. They named two of these after their children. She has written many books. In 1993 she won awards for a book she wrote about her work studying fossils.

**Dong Zhiming** is a paleontologist. A paleontologist is someone who studies fossils to learn about life long ago. He studies the fossils of dinosaurs. He wrote an important book on the dinosaur fossils of China in 1988.

**25.** Choose the correct words to complete the sentences.

| | | | | |
|---|---|---|---|---|
| beaks | teeth | footprint | asteroid | outbreak of disease |
| drought | Chile | China | Iran | Austria |
| Afghanistan | Australia | fossils | tissue | bones |

Edward Cope discovered many species of extinct animals before technology existed to locate _____. Luis and Walter Alvarez proposed the idea that many dinosaurs were wiped out by an _____. Dong Zhiming is a paleontologist who wrote a book about the dinosaur fossils found in _____. Patricia Vickers-Rich's work has focused on animals whose fossils have been found in _____.

# Lesson Check

## Can You Explain It?

Explore Online

1. Take another look at the turtle from the beginning of the lesson. How did this turtle end up in the desert? What can this fossil tell us about the land around it? In your answers to these questions, be sure to do the following:

   • Identify where sea turtles live, how they move, and what this information tells you about the history of this environment.

   • Discuss how the turtle fossil may have become exposed over time.

**EVIDENCE NOTEBOOK** Use the information you've collected in your Evidence Notebook to help you cover each point.

_____

_____

_____

_____

_____

_____

_____

_____

## Checkpoints

2. Choose the word or words to complete the sentence.

   A _____ indicates an aquatic environment once existed in an area.

   | wolf fossil | disrupted |
   | rock formation | fish fossil |
   | layer that is eroded | |

**3.** Choose the correct word to complete the sentence.

> youngest    thickest    oldest

If there are four rock layers, the layer at the bottom is most likely the _____.

**4.** Examine the rock layers. Then answer the question.

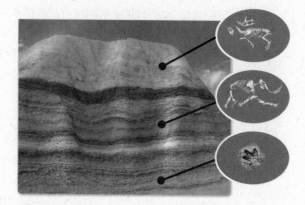

Consider what you can observe in the image. Is there evidence in the image that this environment has changed over time? Make a claim by circling yes or no.

Yes    No

Support your claim by selecting the accurate evidence below.
  **a.** The fossils are all terrestrial, so there is no evidence that an aquatic environment once existed here.
  **b.** There are only five rock layers. This does not provide enough evidence to state whether or not the environment changed.
  **c.** The layers are made of different types of rock. This shows that the environment changed over time.
  **d.** The three fossils shown are different types of animals. This shows that the environment changed over time.

**5.** What can show that the type of environment in an area has changed over time? Circle all that apply.
  **a.** many fossils in different layers of rock
  **b.** fossils from different climates in different layers of rock
  **c.** no fossils in any layers of rock
  **d.** land and water fossils in two layers of rock near each other

**6.** Infer why it could be possible to find the same type of dinosaur fossil in the third rock layer from the top layer in Spain, but in the fifth rock layer from the top layer in England. Select all that apply.
  **a.** It is not possible for one type of fossil to be in different layers.
  **b.** Some rock layers may have eroded in Spain but not England.
  **c.** Dinosaurs are extinct in Spain, but they are not extinct in England.
  **d.** The environments changed at different rates in both locations.

# Lesson Roundup

**A.** Choose the answer that correctly orders the environments represented by the rock layers to the right in order from oldest to youngest.

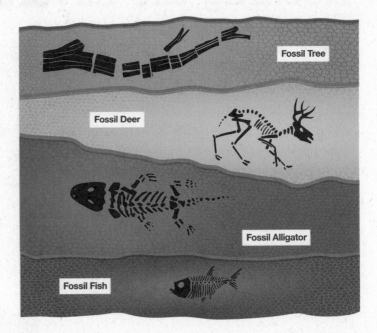

   **a.** lake, swamp, grassland, forest
   **b.** lake, grassland, swamp, forest
   **c.** forest, grassland, swamp, lake
   **d.** forest, swamp, lake, grassland

**B.** What are some limitations of using fossils to learn about past environments? Select all that apply.

   **a.** Fossils are not common in many places.

   **b.** Fossils might indicate more than one type of environment.

   **c.** Fossils do not show enough detail to identify an environment.

   **d.** There are many different types of fossils.

   **e.** Fossils are often missing pieces

**C.** Choose the correct word that completes each sentence.

| earthquakes | fossils | erosion | climate | position |
|---|---|---|---|---|

Rock layers can be disrupted when rock is worn away by _____.

Rock layers have been disrupted. But you can use _____

to tell when two disrupted layers are the same age.

**517**

# Rocking the Layers

Observe the way the rock layers shown have changed. Your task is to research how rock layers can change and identify the processes that made the changes. You should then design a model of the process that formed the rock layers or you can model one of the other processes that change rock layers. As part of your model, you may wish to show how rock layers are formed.

**DEFINE YOUR TASK:** What main question will you need to research?

How have the rock layers changed?

_____

_____

_____

_____

_____

Review the checklist at the end of this Unit Performance Task. Keep those requirements in mind as you proceed.

**RESEARCH:** Use online and library sources to research how rock layers form and are changed. Identify at least three ways rock layers can change. List your findings, and cite your sources.

_____

_____

**BRAINSTORM:** With your team, brainstorm ways to model the rock layer change. Identify three or more ways, then evaluate the ways and choose the best.

_____

_____

_____

**PLAN YOUR PROCEDURE:** Consider the questions below as your group prepares its model. Write a few sentences below to briefly summarize your strategy.

1. What type of model will be used?
2. What type of materials should be used in the model to best represent the natural world?
3. What would the area the rock formation is in look like before and after the changes?
4. Does our model properly represent the area it can be found in?
5. How will the model illustrate the changes in the rock layers?
6. What other areas is this pattern of change in rock layers seen?

_____

_____

_____

_____

_____

_____

_____

_____

**MAKE YOUR MODEL:** Use the materials available to make your model. Label any important information other people might need to see.

**COMMUNICATE:** Present your model to the class. Cite evidence to explain how the rock formation changes over time.

## ✔️ Checklist

**Review your project and check off each completed item.**

_____ Includes evidence that show how rock layers change over time.

_____ Includes any patterns of change seen and how they relate to how rock layers change.

_____ Includes evidence you have found in your research.

_____ Includes a model that shows the way rock layers change.

_____ Includes evidence in the model that supports proof of the changes in the rock layers.

# Unit Review

1.  What is the most reliable way to judge the age of a rock layer? Circle the correct choice.

    **a.** The lower the layer, the older the rock.

    **b.** The higher the layer, the older the rock.

    **c.** The darker the layer, the older the rock.

    **d.** The lighter the layer, the older the rock.

2.  Which of the following may have caused the formation shown here? Circle all that apply.

    **a.** an earthquake

    **b.** delta formation

    **c.** volcanic activity

    **d.** glacier movement

    **e.** underground pressure

3.  Choose the word that best completes each sentence.

    | fossils | glaciers | formations | layers |
    | --- | --- | --- | --- |

    Scientists can determine the age of a rock layer by studying the

    _____ found in that layer.

    _____ of rock can show how an environment has changed

    over time.

**4.** Indicate whether each sentence applies to glaciers, or natural bridges. Write *NB* for natural bridges or *G* for glaciers.

_____ Gravity forms rock into an arch.

_____ Gravity causes huge ice formations.

_____ Loose material inside them erodes away.

_____ Downhill movement creates large grooves.

**5.** Choose from the word bank to complete the sentence.

| ice | sand | water | wildlife |
|-----|------|-------|----------|

The petrified trees in this desert are evidence that there was once

far more _____ in the area.

**6.** Which present-day organism has also been found in fossilized form? Circle the correct choice.

**a.** ferns

**b.** Irish elk

**c.** mosasaurs

**d.** giant short-faced bears

**7.** You find a four-legged fossil. In what type of environment did it most likely live? What evidence from the fossil would support your answer?

_____

_____

_____

This fossil was found in rock high in the mountains.

**8.** What is **most likely** to be true of the region in which this fossil was found?

    **a.** It was once frozen.

    **b.** It was once a desert.

    **c.** It was once a lake.

    **d.** It was once temperate.

**9.** Choose the word that best completes each sentence.

| **insects** | **mammals** | **fish** | **snails** | **ferns** |
|---|---|---|---|---|

Fossils with fins and scales prove that _____ have existed

for millions of years.

Ammonites are extinct, but their fossils show us that they had shells similar to

_____ .

| **water** | **air** | **environment** |
|---|---|---|

**10.** A large variety of fossils are found in a region's different rock layers.

This indicates that the region's _____ has changed several times.

# Natural Resources and Hazards

**Explore Online**

**Unit Project: Resources Debate**
Which nonrenewable energy resources are better for the environment? You will research pros and cons and support your argument with evidence. Ask your teacher for details.

The Japanese town was destroyed by a large, powerful wave called a *tsunami*. A tsunami is a type of destructive natural process that humans cannot prevent.

# At a Glance

## Vocabulary Game: **Bingo**

**Materials**
- 1 set of word cards • 1 bingo board for each player • Game markers such as paper clips

**Set Up** - Players will write a vocabulary word in each square of their bingo board. Words can be written in any order and used more than once.

**Directions**

1. The caller chooses a word card, reads the word aloud, and places the card in a second pile.

2. Players place markers on their bingo boards for the words that are called.

3. Repeat steps 1 and 2 until a player calls "Bingo" with 5 boxes in a row.

4. Check the answers against the chosen cards.

**pollution**

Waste products that damage an ecosystem.

**resources**

Any material that can be used to satisfy a need.

# Unit Vocabulary

 **drawback:** A disadvantage or problem.

 **natural hazard:** An earth process that threatens to harm people and property.

 **natural resource:** Materials found in nature that people and other living things use.

 **nonrenewable resource:** A resource that once used cannot be replaced in a reasonable amount of time.

 **pollution:** Waste products that damage an ecosystem.

 **renewable resource:** A resource that can be replaced within a reasonable amount of time.

 **resource:** Any material that can be used to satisfy a need.

# What Nonrenewable Resources Are Used for Energy?

Oil is buried deep within Earth's surface. In order to remove it, big drills have to dig down into the ground, or even into the ocean floor. Many cars use oil and gasoline, as fuel. Look at the image to learn more.

**By the end of this lesson . . .**
you'll be able to describe nonrenewable resources and explain the effects of using them.

© Houghton Mifflin Harcourt • Image Credits: ©Alberto Incrocci/Photodisc/Getty Images

# Can You Explain It?

The look of cars has changed a lot over time. The way cars run is also starting to change. Many of the first cars were steam cars powered by coal. Many of today's cars run on gasoline.

**1.** The cars in the photos above differ. What factors do you think car designers consider when designing a car that doesn't run on gasoline? What might be a problem of designing such a car?

_____

_____

_____

_____

 **EVIDENCE NOTEBOOK** Look for this icon to help you gather evidence to answer the questions above.

# Materials We Use

## Resources Around You

A **resource** is anything that helps you live. Your house is a resource because it gives you shelter. The clothes you wear are a resource because they help keep you warm. A **natural resource** is a material from nature that people can use. Water, air, trees, wind, fossil fuels, minerals, and sunlight are examples of natural resources.

**2.** Match the text to the picture above by writing in the correct letter in each circle.

**a.** The water you drink comes from a river, a lake, or an underground well.

**b.** The part of the pencil that writes is made of graphite, a mineral.

**c.** Most paper is made from the mashed-up wood of trees.

**d.** Metals are found in Earth's rocky layers.

**e.** Cotton is often used to make curtains. Cotton comes from a plant.

**f.** Plastic is made from petroleum. Petroleum is also known as crude oil, a fossil fuel.

**3.** Explain how three different items you see in your classroom are made from materials found in nature.

_____

_____

_____

# Limited Supply

A **nonrenewable resource** is a resource that, once used, cannot be replaced in a reasonable amount of time. Fossil fuels, such as crude oil, coal, and natural gas, are nonrenewable resources. These fossil fuels are burned to release energy and generate electricity. They are nonrenewable because they take hundreds of millions of years to form.

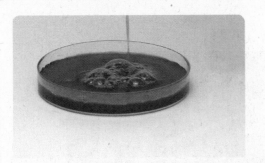

Crude oil is the remains of once-living organisms that were buried under mud. It is used for heat, to fuel vehicles, and is an ingredient of many products, like plastics and paints.

Coal is the buried remains of plants that died millions of years ago. In some places coal is used for heat and for cooking. Some early trains and ships ran on coal.

Natural gas is the remains of once-living organisms. It is used for heat and as a fuel source for buses and other vehicles.

Uranium is a natural element not from organisms but found in rocks formed billions of years ago. Uranium is used to produce nuclear energy. It is a nonrenewable resource, but it is not a fossil fuel.

**4.** How do these nonrenewable resources help people in their daily lives?

_____

_____

**Language SmArts**

## Compare and Contrast

**5.** How are crude oil, coal, and natural gas different from uranium?

_____

_____

# Collecting and Processing

Each picture shows an example of how nonrenewable energy sources are collected or processed. Fossil fuels such as crude oil, coal, and natural gas are first removed from Earth's crust. Then they can be used by electricity generating plants to provide electricity to homes and businesses.

Nonrenewable resources cannot replenish themselves. To make sure people have enough energy for current and future needs, efforts have been made to conserve fossil fuels and use them wisely. The effects of carbon dioxide emissions are another reason why these efforts have been made.

Coal, which is mined from deposits in layers of rocks, is taken to electricity-generating plants to be burned and converted to electrical energy.

Uranium is mined from rocks and is used to create large amounts of energy, which is then provided to homes and businesses for heat and electricity. It is a fuel source for nuclear energy plants.

Gasoline used as fuel in vehicles comes from crude oil, which is drilled from underground wells, including wells that are under water. It is also burned to generate electricity.

Natural gas is extracted from rock formations deep underground and then transported by pipeline and burned for use in electricity generation.

 **HANDS-ON  Apply What You Know**

## The School's Energy

6. Do research to find out about the energy generating plant that supplies electricity to your school. How does it generate electricity? Make a poster about your findings. Compare your findings with your classmates.

## What Do They Use?

**7.** Draw lines to connect the nonrenewable resources with the facilities that use them.

**8.** Choose between natural gas or coal. Describe how this energy source is used in your daily life.

Images Plus/Getty Images

Images/Shutterstock; (bcr) ©Harry Taylor/Dorling Kindersley/Getty Images; (tcl) ©istock/getty Images Plus/Getty Images; (bl) ©Jupiterimages/Getty Images; (tr) ©Dmitriy Sechin/

 **EVIDENCE NOTEBOOK** What kinds of vehicles can you think of that do not run using one of these nonrenewable sources of energy? List your ideas in your Evidence Notebook.

**9.** Do you think energy usage changed in the United States in the 20 years between 1990 and 2010? Use the timeline below and find out.

The amount of energy used is expressed in Btu. Btu stands for British Thermal Unit. Amounts of energy can be measured in Btu. A quadrillion is a huge number. It is 1 followed by 15 zeros. A 100-square-meter home needs around 24,000 Btus to heat in winter.

### 1990
**U.S. population** = 249 million
**Petroleum use** = 34 quadrillion Btu
**Natural gas use** = 20 quadrillion Btu
**Coal use** = 19 quadrillion Btu
**Nuclear energy use** = 6 quadrillion Btu
**Other renewable energy use** = 1 quadrillion Btu

### 1995
**U.S. population** = 261 million
**Petroleum use** = 35 quadrillion Btu
**Natural gas use** = 23 quadrillion Btu
**Coal use** = 20 quadrillion Btu
**Nuclear energy use** = 7 quadrillion Btu
**Other renewable energy use** = 2 quadrillion Btu

### 2000
**U.S. population** = 281 million
**Petroleum use** = 38 quadrillion Btu
**Natural gas use** = 24 quadrillion Btu
**Coal use** = 22 quadrillion Btu
**Nuclear energy use** = 5 quadrillion Btu
**Other renewable energy use** = 2 quadrillion Btu

### 2005
**U.S. population** = 296 million
**Petroleum use** = 40 quadrillion Btu
**Natural gas use** = 23 quadrillion Btu
**Coal use** = 23 quadrillion Btu
**Nuclear energy use** = 8 quadrillion Btu
**Other renewable energy use** = 2 quadrillion Btu

### 2010
**U.S. population** = 309 million
**Petroleum use** = 36 quadrillion Btu
**Natural gas use** = 24 quadrillion Btu
**Coal use** = 21 quadrillion Btu
**Nuclear energy use** = 8 quadrillion Btu
**Other renewable energy use** = 4 quadrillion Btu

10. Choose one of the resources from the timeline, and graph how its use changed over time.

_____

Units of resources used

Year

11. Does the data in the timeline support the statements below? If it does, circle *true*. If it doesn't, circle *false*.

Coal use in the United States decreased about 2 quadrillion Btu between 2005 and 2010.

true     false

Renewable energy use increased between 1990 and 2010.

true     false

## Putting It Together

12. Write the word or phrase that correctly completes each sentence.

> fossil fuels     nonrenewable     electricity-generating plants
> resources     renewable     generators

All living things need _____ in order to live. Some of these exist naturally

all around us and are called natural resources. Some natural resources are considered

_____ because they cannot be replaced in a reasonable amount of time.

Examples of nonrenewable resources include _____, such as coal,  crude

oil, and natural gas.

# Search and Find

## Digging a Little Deeper

Nonrenewable resources are being used at a much faster rate than they can be replenished, or replaced. Today, there is more demand for coal and crude oil than there was before. Due to crude oil being used up, big drills called oil rigs dig deeper into the ground to find crude oil. People now need to dig deep or strip away the surface of the earth to reach coal.

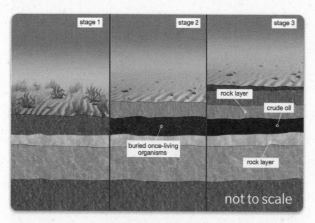

Crude oil formed from small once-living organisms that died million years ago. Pressure and heat from rock layers above the buried once-living organisms formed crude oil.

Today, mechanical drills dig deep into Earth's rock layers to remove crude oil and natural gas. Natural gas is a by-product of both crude oil and coal. It forms along both of these fossil fuels.

Coal formed from plants that died millions of years ago. Over time, the plants were squeezed and heated by the layers of rock pushing down from above.

Today, surface and underground mines are used to remove the coal.

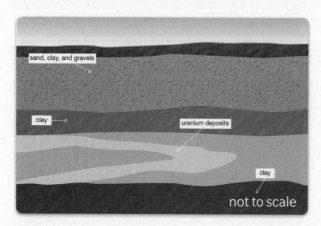

Uranium is an element found in certain rocks and rock layers. It is removed by surface mining or by deep underground mining.

It can also be removed from rocks by leaching, fusing water and chemicals to release it from rock.

Before the 20th century, people relied mainly on wood—and some—coal for heating and cooking. Burning coal started the industrial age with the development of steam engines that fueled trains and other machines and electricity-generating plants. Cars and other engines increased the use of crude oil as a source of energy. As technology improved, people found ways to mine and use natural gas and nuclear energy.

## How to Get It

**13.** Identify how each type of nonrenewable resource is mined. Write the letters on the lines. Some lines will contain more than one letter.

_____

_____

**a.** underground mines

**b.** surface mines

**c.** drilling

**d.** leaching

_____

_____

### Language SmArts
# Summarize

**14.** What do the methods of extracting these fuels all have in common?

_____

_____

_____

_____

**Tip**

The English Language Arts Handbook can provide help with understanding how to summarize.

# Where Are They Found?

Scientists and engineers use special nonrenewable resource technology to locate, remove, and process coal, crude oil, natural gas, and uranium. Each of these methods has certain benefits and risks. Some create **pollution**, or waste products that damage an ecosystem.

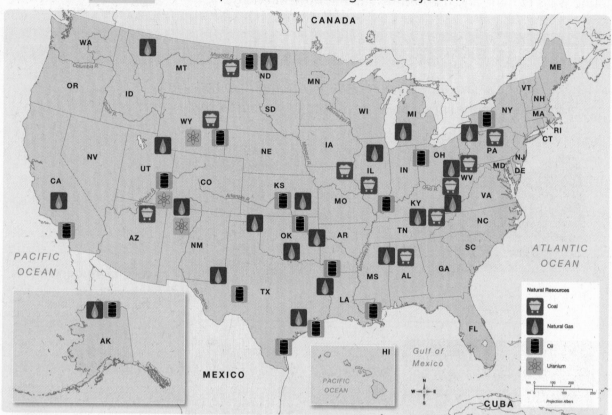

 In the United States, crude oil is found mostly in the Midwest, South, Southwest, Alaska, and around Pennsylvania.

 Natural gas is found mostly in Alaska, Texas, Oklahoma, New Mexico, Wyoming, and Louisiana. Some can also be found in the Midwest.

 The Midwest, Montana, Wyoming, and Pennsylvania are the main sources of coal in the United States.

 The United States was once the leader in uranium mining. Today, however, uranium is mined in only a few places, including New Mexico, Utah and Wyoming.

15. Choose the word or phrase that correctly completes each sentence.

| crude oil | coal | natural gas | uranium | Wyoming | Pennsylvania |

Natural gas, _____, and coal can be found in the Midwest. Natural gas and uranium can be found in New Mexico and _____. Oklahoma has both _____ and crude oil. Pennsylvania is one of the main sources of _____ in the United States.

**16.** Write *u* for uranium, *o* for oil, *c* for coal, or *g* for gas to identify the nonrenewable resource shown being used in each picture below.

Many kitchen stoves cook food with an open flame. A fossil fuel is piped into the stove, where it ignites and heats up the food.

Early trains had steam engines. A fire heated up water, which turned to steam. The steam then helped the trains to move.

Paint is a product of fossil fuels. The same product that is used in paint is also used in plastic, rubber, and soap.

**Kitchen stove**

**Train**

**Paint**

**HANDS-ON  Apply What You Know**

# Mining Challenge

**17.** Model a mining operation. The beads and sunflower seeds represent minerals. You will be using a spoon to "mine" minerals by making neat piles of each. Once time is up, count up the number of gold, silver, and blue beads, and sunflower seeds "mined". Multiply those numbers by their values.  Then, add all your totals together. Lastly, subtract the cost of any white beads "mined" from your total value of what you "mined". Did you make a profit?

**Materials**
- 1 spoon
- 1 pan
- birdseeds
- beads:

**Value**
- gold bead = $5
- silver bead = $4
- blue bead = $3
- sunflower seed = $2

**Cost**
- white bead = $100 each (reclamation)

_____

_____

_____

_____

**EVIDENCE NOTEBOOK**  What are some pros and cons of cars that run on gasoline? List your ideas in your evidence notebook.

# Pros and Cons

The pros and cons of something are similar to its benefits and risks. The pros are the positive things about it and the cons are the negative things, or **drawbacks**. Using fossil fuels has some pros and some cons. A *pro* is that they give us affordable fuel. A *con* is that using them often causes pollution, or harmful substances mixed with water, air, or soil.

Humans have used coal for energy for thousands of years. Some forms of strip-mining for coal harm ecosytems.

Many vehicles run on gasoline. Hazardous oil spills have occurred when transporting crude oil.

Airplanes use fossil fuel to run their engines. This fuel is expensive and also adds pollution to the air.

Burning fossil fuels in cars and at electricity-generating plants generates energy, but it also creates pollution and harmful gases in Earth's atmosphere.

Burning natural gas and using nuclear energy produce less pollution than other fossil fuels, but transporting uranium is dangerous.

**18.** Write the letter of the sentence that completes the chart.

| Cause | Effect |
|---|---|
|  | Pollution and harmful gases are added to the air. |
| New nuclear plants are built. |  |
|  | Habitats and farmland are lost. |
| Crude oil is transported. |  |

**a.** Uranium is rare and must be moved long distances.

**b.** Fossil fuels are burned.

**c.** Oil spills pollute water and destroy wildlife.

**d.** Resources are surface mined.

# Hybrid Cars

Hybrid cars use two or more different methods to generate energy to run the car. There are different types of hybrid cars. Some newer hybrid cars can run on both gas and electric combined. The image below shows a standard hybrid.

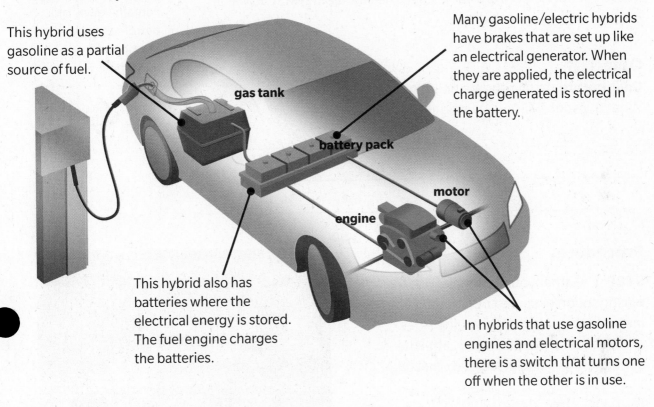

This hybrid uses gasoline as a partial source of fuel.

gas tank

battery pack

Many gasoline/electric hybrids have brakes that are set up like an electrical generator. When they are applied, the electrical charge generated is stored in the battery.

motor

engine

This hybrid also has batteries where the electrical energy is stored. The fuel engine charges the batteries.

In hybrids that use gasoline engines and electrical motors, there is a switch that turns one off when the other is in use.

19. How does a hybrid car such as the one in the diagram help with some of the cons of fossil fuel use?

_____

_____

Language SmArts

# Making Inferences

20. Some cars run entirely on electric energy. How do you think their batteries might be recharged with electricity?

_____

_____

_____

Tip

The English Language Arts Handbook can provide help with understanding how to make inferences.

# HANDS-ON ACTIVITY
# Catch That Dirt

Tiny dirt and dust particles are floating in the air around us. Some places have more of these tiny particles than others. Perhaps the air inside your classroom is cleaner than the air outside. Maybe the air outside is cleaner.

**Materials**
- 4 small plastic containers with lids
- petroleum jelly
- plastic spoon
- hand lens

## Objective

**Collaborate** to investigate pollution in the air.
What question will you investigate to meet this objective?

_____

_____

_____

## Procedure

**STEP 1** Gather your materials. Use the plastic spoon to spread petroleum jelly inside each container. Cover the sides and bottom with a thin layer. Label the containers 1–4 and place a lid on each.

Why do you think you have prepared more than one container?

_____

_____

_____

**STEP 2** Look closely at all four containers. Describe what the inside surface of the containers looks like.

_____

_____

_____

_____

_____

540

© Houghton Mifflin Harcourt

**STEP 3** Place two containers indoors. Remove the lids.

Place the other two containers outdoors. Remove the lids. Leave the containers in place for two hours. Write the location of each container.

_____

_____

_____

_____

**STEP 4** After two hours, use a hand lens to study the inside of each container.

Describe what you see on the insides of the containers.

**Container 1:** _____

_____

_____

_____

_____

**Container 2:** _____

_____

_____

_____

**Container 3:** _____

_____

_____

_____

**Container 4:** _____

_____

_____

## Analyze Your Results

**STEP 5**  Did you notice differences between the containers? If you did, describe them.

_____

_____

_____

**STEP 6**  Share and compare your results with other students. Discuss how you could explain the differences you observed.

_____

_____

_____

## Draw Conclusions

**STEP 7**  Based on your observations, which containers were left to sit in the cleaner air?

_____

_____

**STEP 8**  Make a claim about the air inside your classroom and the air outside. Cite evidence to support your claim.

_____

_____

_____

**STEP 9**  What does this investigation tell you about the environment?

_____

_____

_____

**STEP 10**  Think of other questions you want to ask about air quality.

_____

_____

_____

# Discover More

**Check out this path . . . or go online to choose one of these other paths.**

| Careers in Science & Engineering | • What's Around You? • On a Mining Mission |

## Types of "-ISTs"

 Explore Online

As we use up nonrenewable fossil fuel supplies, the need for alternative energy resources, such as solar, wind, or biodiesel, increases. Many different kinds of scientists do work that can be related to fossil fuels. Some discover. Some invent.

A petroleum geologist locates and discovers places where new fossil fuel deposits can be found.

A chemist might investigate how chemicals found in fossil fuels can be used as fuel and to make products.

**21.** Decide if each description is a discovery or an invention. Match each to the scientist who was most likely responsible for it.

**a.** located deposits of crude oil in North Dakota

**b.** used technology to inform other experts where to drill

**c.** developed new types of sunglasses

**d.** invented new superglue

**e.** stopped underwater oil spill

petroleum geologist

chemist

A climatologist studies long-term changes in climate. These changes are related to use of fossil fuels.

Marine biologists describe the effects of fossil fuel pollution on the plants and animals living in the ocean.

**22.** Describe a similarity and difference among the four different types of scientists.

_____

_____

_____

**23.** Pick your favorite type of scientist from the ones described here. Research interesting facts about that type of scientist's job.

Which type of scientist did you choose, and why?

_____

_____

_____

**24.** Describe where that type of scientist does most of his or her work.

_____

_____

**25.** Compare your research with that of a classmate who researched a different type of scientist's job.

Which job would you rather have? Why?

_____

_____

_____

# Lesson Check

Name _____

## Can You Explain It?

1. Think back to the cars at the beginning of the lesson. Now that you've learned about resources, explain how vehicles in use today relate to the available fuel resources. Be sure to do the following:

   • Identify the types of fuel source.

   • Tell whether fuel sources are renewable or nonrenewable.

   • Identify technologies that engineers build into things to replace fossil fuels.

   • Identify the benefits and drawbacks of each fuel source used.

**EVIDENCE NOTEBOOK** Use the information you've collected in your Evidence Notebook to help you cover each point above.

_____

_____

_____

_____

_____

_____

_____

_____

_____

## Checkpoints

2. Which of the following is a nonrenewable resource not made from fossil fuels?

   **a.** natural gas        **c.** uranium

   **b.** oil                **d.** coal

**3.** Write the letter that identifies each nonrenewable energy resource.

    **a.** natural gas

    **b.** coal

    **c.** uranium

    **d.** crude oil

**4.** Write the words or phrases that make each sentence correct.

| | | |
|---|---|---|
| **inexpensive** | **decreasing quickly** | **increasing quickly** |
| **increasing slowly** | **hundreds of thousands** | **hundreds of millions** |

Fossil fuels were once easy to find and _____ to use because there was so much of each available. But today, we are using so much that supplies are _____. It took _____ of years for fossil fuels to form, so there will be no more when our current supply is gone.

**5.** What will most likely cause the use of fossil fuels to decrease over the next hundred years? Circle all that apply.

    **a.** steep increase in price of fossil fuels

    **c.** availability of alternate energy fuels

    **b.** higher need for fossil fuels

    **d.** lower price of fossil fuels.

**6.** Write *renewable* or *nonrenewable* to complete the sentence.

Fuels that takes millions of years to develop are _____.

# Lesson Roundup

**A.** Write the letter for each nonrenewable resource by its description.

| a. solid     b. nonrenewable     c. used to generate electricity     d. fossil fuel |

_____    _____    _____

**B.** Which statement describes a benefit of buying an electric car instead of a gasoline-fueled car? Circle the correct answer.

   **a.** Electric cars are bigger.

   **b.** Electric cars are easier to drive.

   **c.** Electric cars are less expensive.

   **d.** Electric cars cause less air pollution.

**Extraction of Fossil Fuels**

**C.** What could explain why an oil rig is no longer able to get crude oil from an area?

   **a.** The oil has become solid.

   **b.** All the oil has been removed.

   **c.** The drill needs to be replaced.

   **d.** The oil has moved to a different area.

**D.** Keep track of anything else you learned about extracting fossil fuels here!

_____

_____

_____

**E.** Circle the sources of energy that are are the remains of once-living organisms.

   **a.** uranium

   **b.** coal.

   **c.** natural gas

   **d.** crude oil

# What Renewable Resources Are Used for Energy?

A wind farm is a place where several turbines are installed to convert wind to electrical energy.

**By the end of this lesson . . .**
you'll be able to explain the potential risks and benefits of using wind, water, and solar energy compared to fossil fuels.

© Houghton Mifflin Harcourt • Image Credits: ©Lurlyu/iStock/Getty Images Plus/Getty Image

# Can You Explain It?

Look carefully at this house. Even though it's not close to any town, it still has electricity. When you look at most houses, you see wires connected to them. Wires bring electricity to the house so the refrigerator, lights, TV, heating and cooling system, and other electric appliances work. Some houses have underground wires, while others get their electricity from other sources.

**1.** This home has plenty of electricity day and night. How does it get most of its electricity?

_____

_____

_____

_____

_____

_____

_____

_____

_____

**Tip**

To recall what you have read about energy, read What Is Energy? and How Is Energy Transferred?

 **EVIDENCE NOTEBOOK** Look for this icon to help you gather evidence to answer the question above.

# Exploring Renewable Resources

## Use It Again

As you have learned, nonrenewable resources cannot be replenished in a reasonable amount of time. However, **renewable resources** are resources that can be replenished within a reasonable amount of time. They are used to generate electricity. They were the main forms of energy used before the 20th century.

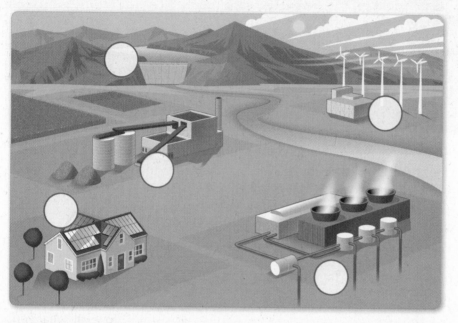

2. Read below to learn more about renewable energy sources. Then, match the text to the picture by writing the correct letter in each circle.

**a.** Using wind as an energy source does not produce pollution. It has low or no cost. Because we will never run out of wind, it is renewable.

**b.** Solar energy is clean, renewable energy from the sun. When solar panels capture energy from the sun and change it to electricity, no pollution is given off.

**c.** The energy of water flowing through a dam is called hydroelectricty. Hydroelectric dams use water, which is a renewable resource.

**d.** Geothermal-fueled plants use the heat below Earth's surface to produce electricity. Earth's heat is a renewable resource.

**e.** Biomass is fuel that comes from dead organisms. The most common type is wood. Other types include cornstalks and animal waste. When burned, it is used to generate electricity.

3. What is the difference between a renewable and a nonrenewable resource?

_____

_____

_____

# How Does That Work?

**4.** When you turn on the TV or a light bulb in a lamp, you're using electricity. Draw a line to match the electricity-producing device to the natural resource.

 **EVIDENCE NOTEBOOK** Do any of the nonrenewable resources you have learned about seem as if they might be what's providing electricity to the house you saw at the beginning of the lesson? Record your thoughts and observations in your Evidence Notebook.

 Language SmArts
## Making Connections

**5.** Describe two renewable and two nonrenewable resources where you live. What are the natural resources and the electricity-producing devices?

_____

_____

_____

# Energy Plants

Each photo shows one type of renewable energy, and how it is used to produce electricity that people can use instead of nonrenewable resources for energy needs.

 Explore Online

Wind energy does not pollute the air. Wind spins the blades of huge turbines. The spinning blades turn a device, called a generator, inside the turbine. The generator spins to produce electricity.

Hydroelectric energy is fueled by water, a clean energy source. Hydroelectric plants are dams with machinery inside. Water flows through the dam, turning the blades of a turbine. The turbine then spins a generator, producing electricity.

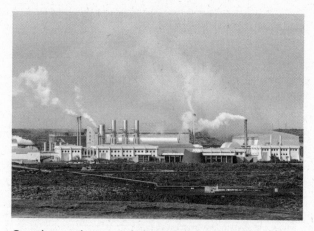

Geothermal energy is heat from the earth. Geothermal plants use steam from underground to spin the blades of a turbine. The turbine spins a generator that makes an electric current. It is considered a clean fuel source, because once the steam is used, it is pumped back into the ground.

Solar energy is considered to be clean energy. Each solar panel contains several dozen solar cells. These are devices that turn the sun's energy into electricity though a chemical reaction.

**6.** Choose two energy sources from the ones you learned about. How are the processes to produce energy alike? How are they different?

_____

_____

_____

# Tidal Energy

Scientists and engineers are working on tapping other sources of renewable energy. Tidal energy is one example.

Gravity helps produce tides—the predictable rise-and-fall action of the ocean. Huge amounts of seawater flow over the ocean floor in between tides. By anchoring turbines in areas of the ocean floor where tidal flow is especially strong, electricity can be produced.

AK1000 is the world's largest tidal turbine. Its rotors have a diameter of 18 meters (60 feet) and will harness enough tidal energy to generate electricity for more than 1,000 homes.

**7.** What do you think the engineering challenges are in building turbines that operate in the sea?

_____

_____

_____

_____

**EVIDENCE NOTEBOOK** Have you identified any sources of energy that could provide electricity to the house without being visible from the outside? Record your findings in your Evidence Notebook.

## Putting It Together

**8.** Test your knowledge of renewable resources by completing the questions below.

| burned | replaced | used | solar | biomass | geothermal |
|--------|----------|------|-------|---------|------------|
| dams | generators | turbines | water | wind | ice |

Choose the correct words that complete each sentence.

Renewable energy sources are those that can be _____ in a

reasonable amount of time. Energy from the sun is called _____ energy.

Machines called _____ use the wind to produce energy. Hydroelectricity

uses moving _____ to produce electricity.

# Renewable Natural Resources

## Cloudy Days, No Wind, Little Water

If you stand in the middle of a vegetable farm, you'll see rows of crops. If you stand in the middle of a wind farm, you'll see rows of wind turbines. Wind farms are built in very windy areas. The wind makes the turbines spin, which produces electricity. Moving water can also make turbines spin, which produces electricity. The electricity from these devices goes to an electricity-generating plant and then to homes and businesses.

Electricity from solar energy can come from large fields of solar panels and through an electricity-generating plant, too. Solar panels can also be installed directly onto houses.

Energy can be stored for use at times when the wind dies down or there is no sun, or other forms of energy can be used. When there's no wind or sun, backup sources of energy are used to meet people's energy needs. That way, no one is left without electricity.

### Solar, Wind, and Water Energy

Explore Online

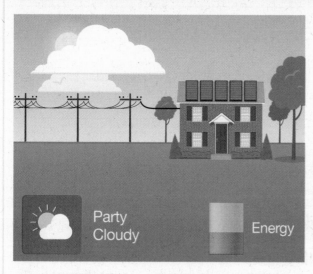

solar panels

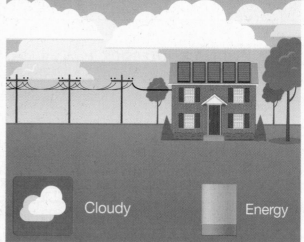

solar panels

**9.** What can you conclude from the images of solar panels?

_____

_____

_____

_____

© Houghton Mifflin Harcourt

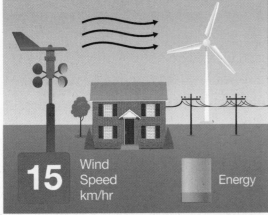

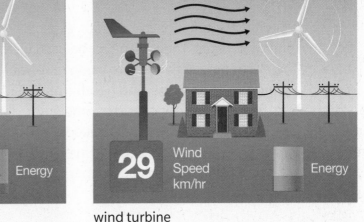

wind turbine

wind turbine

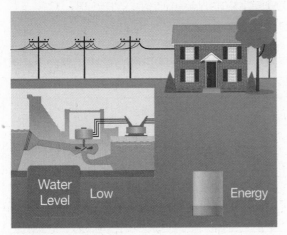

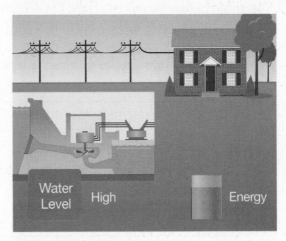

hydroelectric dam

hydroelectric dam

**10.** Which of the following best describe the relationship between water and energy in a hydroelectric dam? Circle all that apply.

**a.** More water moving through the dam means less energy.

**b.** More water moving through the dam means more energy.

**c.** Less water moving through the dam means more energy.

**d.** Less water moving through the dam means less energy

**11.** Based on the pictures you see here and on the previous page, what do you think are the benefits and drawbacks of using renewable energy sources?

_____

_____

_____

 **EVIDENCE NOTEBOOK** Do you think renewable sources of energy can generate electricity for a house by themselves, or are other sources of energy necessary? Record evidence in your Evidence Notebook.

# Benefits and Drawbacks

Renewable energy resources have benefits, especially when compared with nonrenewable energy sources. They will never be used up and do not pollute the air. However, there are some drawbacks to using renewable energy sources.

Solar panels, hydroelectric dams, and geothermal plants can be expensive to build or set up. Both wind turbines and hydroelectric dams can harm wildlife. Biomass plants and geothermal plants can cause some pollution the air. Hyroelectric dams can cause habitat loss and even flood valuable land. However, they still cause less pollution to the air in comparison to nonrenewable energy sources, and they will never run out.

**12.** The table below shows the benefits and drawbacks of five different types of renewable energy sources. Fill in the source for each type of energy.

> **hydroelectric dam**　**solar panels**　**biomass plant**　**wind turbines**　**geothermal plant**

| Source | Benefits | Drawbacks |
|---|---|---|
| | • clean energy source<br>• will never be used up | • habitat loss<br>• can harm wildlife<br>• floods valuable land<br>• expensive to build or set up |
| | • clean energy source<br>• will never be used up | • can harm wildlife<br>• can be noisy and unattractive<br>• only works well on windy days |
| | • clean energy source<br>• will never be used up | • expensive to build or set up<br>• only works well on sunny days |
| | • will never be used up | • can be used in a limited number of places<br>• can pollute air<br>• expensive to build or set up |
| | • will never be used up<br>• reduces waste that goes to landfills | • can pollute air |

**13.** Which benefits do all renewable sources of energy share? Select all that apply.

  **a.** Their waste is easy to clean up.

  **b.** Energy from renewable sources is cleaner than energy from nonrenewable resources.

  **c.** They will never be used up.

  **d.** They work well in all environments.

# Going Green Debate

Energy efficiency means to use products or technologies that perform the same function but consume less energy. For example, a compact fluorescent bulb is more energy efficient than a traditional incandescent bulb. It uses much less electrical energy to produce the same amount of light. How do you think renewable and nonrenewable resources compare? Which one do you think is more energy efficient?

**14.** Consider both types of energy resources, then fill out the table below.

- Under *Claim,* fill in either "renewable" or "nonrenewable" to complete the sentence.

- Then under *Evidence,* give three facts that support your claim.

- Use facts from this lesson and the previous one. Research any other facts you need to use as evidence.

| Claim |
|---|
| I think that _____ energy is the most efficient type of energy. |
| **Evidence** |
| a. _____ <br> _____ <br> b. _____ <br> _____ <br> c. _____ <br> _____ |

**15.** Discuss your answer with a classmate. Do you agree or disagree with his or her answer? Explain why or why not.

_____

_____

## Do the Math

# Bright Savings

**16.** Think about the light bulbs in your home. Chances are, you'll see a variety of types. The most common are called incandescent light bulbs. Newer types, such as compact fluorescent bulbs, are more efficient and use less energy.

Use the chart to learn more.

| | High-efficiency incandescent 43 watt | Compact fluorescent 15 watt |
|---|---|---|
| | | |
| **Average number of hours it lasts** | 2,000 | 10,000 |
| **Typical yearly cost** | $3.50 | $1.20 |
| **Benefits** | • uses less electricity than regular incandescent bulbs<br><br>• less air and water pollution from fossil fuel plants that supply most electricity<br><br>• last longer than regular incandescent bulbs, so less use of resources to make them | • uses less electricity than high-efficiency incandescent bulbs, which means less use of fossil fuels that produce most electricity<br><br>• less air and water pollution from electricity-generating plants |
| **Drawbacks** | • burns hotter than regular incandescent bulbs | • contain a small amount of poisonous mercury that they can release when broken or thrown out in regular garbage |

**17.** Have you seen high-efficiency, incandescent, or compact fluorescent bulbs in your home? Which would you choose to use?

_____

_____

_____

**18.** Compare the cost of a high-efficiency incandescent bulb and a compact fluorescent bulb. Use the space above to solve the problem, and then select the best answer.

**a.** The high-efficiency incandescent bulb costs two times as much as the compact fluorescent bulb.

**b.** The high-efficiency incandescent bulb costs about three times as much as the compact fluorescent bulb.

**c.** The high-efficiency incandescent bulb costs almost five times as much as the compact fluorescent bulb.

**d.** The high-efficiency incandescent bulb costs six times as much as the compact fluorescent bulb.

**19.** How many hours longer will the compact fluorescent last compared to the high-efficiency incandescent bulb? Use the space above to solve the problem, and then select the best answer.

**a.** The compact fluorescent bulb will last 2,000 hours longer.

**b.** The compact fluorescent bulb will last 4,000 hours longer.

**c.** The compact fluorescent bulb will last 8,000 hours longer.

**d.** The compact fluorescent bulb will last 10,000 hours longer.

## Plastics from Plants

In the previous lesson, you learned about typical plastics such as PET, or polyethylene terephthalate, which are made from petroleum (oil), a fossil fuel. PET is the most common type of plastic. Did you know we now have ways to make plastics from plants?

### Procedure

**a.** Place 1 tablespoon of cornstarch in the plastic bag.

**b.** Add 1 tablespoon of water.

**c.** Add 2 drops of corn oil.

**d.** Add 2 drops of food coloring.

**e.** Seal the bag almost completely closed. Tilt the bag so the contents settle in one corner, then squish them together to mix.

**f.** Your teacher will place the contents of the bag into a microwave safe container and then place the container in the microwave oven for 20 seconds.

**g.** Your teacher will remove the container from the microwave oven and let it cool before removing the contents.

**h.** Shape the "plastic" with your fingers.

**i.** After working with the plastic for a few minutes, dip it in water.

### Materials

- zip-top plastic bag
- measuring spoons
- 2 drops of food coloring
- 2 drops of corn oil
- 1 tablespoon of cornstarch
- 1 tablespoon of water
- microwave oven
- microwave safe container

**20.** Think about how simple it was to take a few different corn-based ingredients and turn them into a substance you could work into different shapes. Think also about what happened when you dipped the corn plastic into water. How do you think corn plastic compares to petroleum-based plastics in terms of environmental impact?

_____

_____

_____

_____

# Solar Energy!

**21.** Solar energy has many different uses. Write what solar energy is being used for on the line below each picture.

_____

_____

_____

_____

_____

_____

_____

_____

Photography/Alamy (bl) ©Michele Cornelius/Getty Images (br) ©Katja Kircher/Maskot/ Getty Images

## Language SmArts

# Cause and Effect

**Tip**

The English Language Arts Handbook can provide help with understanding cause and effect.

**22.** Choose the best words to complete each sentence.

> **microwaves   pollution   electricity   generator   turbine   fan**

Most renewable energy sources do not cause _____.

Rooftop solar panels turn sunlight into _____. Wind

spins the blades of a _____ to make electricity.

561

# Running on Sunshine

## Objective

Imagine you are going on a camping trip. It is a remote spot. You don't have a battery-powered stove. The weather has been very dry, and the park has banned campfires. You are not allowed to make a cooking fire. You remember that the sun gives off light that generates heat and decide to build a solar hot water heater to bring on the trip. You have a budget of $10.

| Materials | Budgeted materials |
|---|---|
| • water container | • cardboard box—$5 |
| • scissors | • black paint—$3 |
| • tape | • black construction paper—$2 |
| • thermometer | • plastic wrap—$1 |
| • timer or watch | • packing peanuts—$2 |
| • measuring cup | • newspaper—$1 |
| | • cotton balls—$1 |
| | • aluminum foil—$3 |
| | • wax paper—$2 |
| | • paper plates—$1 |
| | • plastic shopping bags—$1 |
| | • paper towels—$1 |

**Collaborate** to design a solar hot water heater.

**Find a Problem:** What question will you investigate to meet this objective?

_____

_____

## Procedure

**STEP 1 Brainstorm:** Think about which materials you can use that will help you capture solar energy. Think about how the color and texture of the materials affects your design. Brainstorm as many ideas as you can think of. Keep in mind your criteria and constraints:

| Criteria | Constraints |
|---|---|
| ☐ Your solar heater should be able to heat at least one cup of water at least 2 °C. | ☐ You may only use the materials your teacher provides. |
| ☐ The heater has to stay warm when it is out of the sunlight, too. | ☐ Your design must be built in the time given. |
| ☐ The heater has to use sunlight to heat the water. | ☐ You must stay within the $10 budget. |

**STEP 2  Plan:** With your group, plan your design. Work together to draw a model of your solar water heater on a separate sheet of paper, and make a materials list suited to your design. Have your teacher approve your design. Gather your materials. What is the problem you need to solve?

_____

_____

_____

_____

_____

**STEP 3  Build:** Build your solar water heater. Draw the finished solar water heater in the box below and label each of its parts. Explain what it does on the lines below.

_____

_____

_____

**STEP 4** **Test:** Test your heater outside. Fill a cup with water. Use the thermometer to record the starting temperature of the water. Record the temperature in the table on the next page, in the "Temperature in the sun" row under 0. Place the heater in bright sunlight. Place the water in the heater. Record the temperature of the water every 5 minutes for 20 minutes in the "Temperature in the sun" row of the table.

How will you know whether your results are accurate? What steps can you take to assure your measurements are accurate?

_____

_____

_____

_____

_____

**STEP 5** Take the heater inside. Measure the temperature of the water right away. Then record it in the "Temperature when not in the sun" row under 0. Then measure and record the water temperature every 5 minutes for the next 20 minutes.

What differences do you notice when moving the heater inside?

_____

_____

_____

_____

_____

**STEP 6** Record the temperatures measured during the investigation in the table below.

| Solar Water Heater Results | | | | | |
|---|---|---|---|---|---|
| Time (min) | 0 | 5 | 10 | 15 | 20 |
| Temperature in the sun (°C) | | | | | |
| Temperature when not in the sun (°C) | | | | | |

## Analyze Your Results

**STEP 7** What was the highest water temperature you recorded? What was the difference between that temperature and your starting temperature?

_____

_____

_____

_____

_____

**STEP 8** Did your heater maintain its temperature when you took it inside? How much did the temperature drop in the 20 minutes it was out of sunlight?

_____

_____

_____

_____

_____

## Analyze Your Results

**STEP 9** **Evaluate and Redesign:** Why did you choose the materials you used? Do you think they helped your heater work? If not, which materials could you use instead? What would you do differently to improve your design?

_____

_____

_____

_____

**STEP 10** Can you claim that your design met the criteria? Why or why not?

_____

_____

## Draw Conclusions

**STEP 11** What evidence do you have that your solar water heater was successful? Did it hold in heat? Explain your answer.

_____

_____

**STEP 12** How do you think you could have made your heater better? What other materials would you have chosen instead?

_____

_____

_____

**STEP 13** **Communicate:** Compare your results to those of the other groups in your class. Did their heaters work better than yours? Why or why not?

_____

_____

_____

**STEP 14** What questions do you have about using solar energy for heat?

_____

_____

# Discover More

**Check out this path . . . or go online to choose one of these other paths.**

| People in Science & Engineering | • Sort It Out<br>• The Hoover Dam |

## Elon Musk

Elon Musk is a successful businessman and physicist who has founded several companies. He is known for the company Tesla Motors. In 2003, the company began work on producing electric cars. The cars run on lithium ion batteries and go about 250 miles before needing to be recharged.

**Elon Musk**

In 2013, Musk announced a new idea called the Hyperloop. The Hyperloop is a transportation idea in which people ride in pods through interconnected tubes. The Hyperloop would run on solar energy and move at speeds of 700 miles per hour.

**A Tesla car**

The Tesla Powerwall is a rechargable lithium-ion battery made for home use. It stores electricity and can provide backup electricity in case of an outage. It can save up to 20 percent on a home's electric bill.

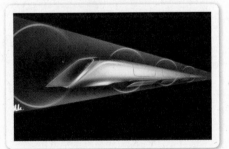

**The Hyperloop**

**A Tesla Powerwall**

**23.** The batteries for electric cars need to be plugged into a source of electricity to be recharged. Which type of energy resource would be better to use to recharge an electric car battery—nonrenewable energy resources or renewable energy resources?

_____

_____

# The History of Cars and Batteries

Most cars today run on fossil fuels such as gasoline and diesel fuel. It is possible, however, for cars to run on electricity alone. Electric cars are not common, but they are becoming more popular.

This timeline shows some important events in the development of electric cars and the batteries that help them run.

## Development of Electric Car Batteries and Cars

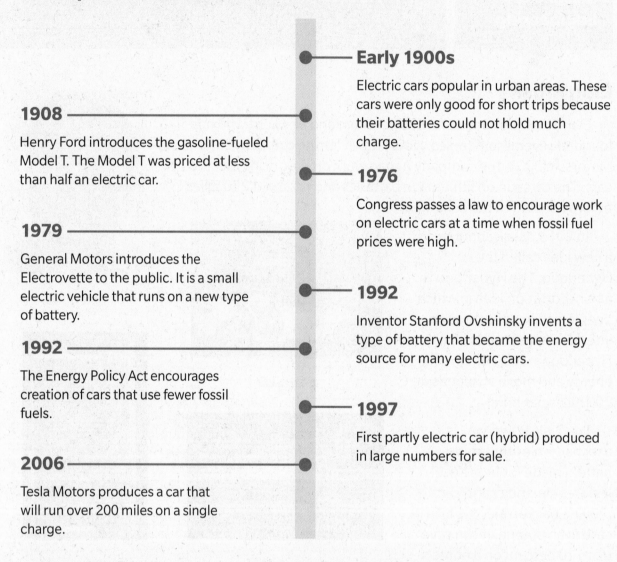

**Early 1900s**

Electric cars popular in urban areas. These cars were only good for short trips because their batteries could not hold much charge.

**1908**

Henry Ford introduces the gasoline-fueled Model T. The Model T was priced at less than half an electric car.

**1976**

Congress passes a law to encourage work on electric cars at a time when fossil fuel prices were high.

**1979**

General Motors introduces the Electrovette to the public. It is a small electric vehicle that runs on a new type of battery.

**1992**

Inventor Stanford Ovshinsky invents a type of battery that became the energy source for many electric cars.

**1992**

The Energy Policy Act encourages creation of cars that use fewer fossil fuels.

**1997**

First partly electric car (hybrid) produced in large numbers for sale.

**2006**

Tesla Motors produces a car that will run over 200 miles on a single charge.

24. What is one thing that has changed about electric car batteries between the early 1900s and 2006? Support your answer with evidence from the timeline.

_____

_____

_____

# Lesson Check

Name _____

## Can You Explain It?

1. Remember the house you saw at the start of
   the lesson? Most houses have wires connected
   to them that bring electricity for people to use
   day and night. How does this house get its
   electricity? Consider the following:

   • evidence of how the house is getting energy
     in the form of electricity

   • wires and other things that are necessary
     to send electricity to a house from an
     electricity-generating plant

   • potential downsides to how this house gets
     its electricity

**EVIDENCE NOTEBOOK** Use the information you've collected in your Evidence
Notebook to help you cover each point above.

_____

_____

_____

_____

_____

_____

_____

_____

## Checkpoints

Choose the correct answer.

2. A family wants to use a renewable energy resource to help provide electricity
   to their house. Which of these energy resources should they use?
   **a.** oil          **b.** solar          **c.** coal          **d.** natural gas

**3.** A new electricity generating plant wants to avoid using any nonrenewable energy resources to produce electricity. Which energy resource should the plant not use?

    **a.** solar

    **b.** geothermal

    **c.** hydroelectric

    **d.** natural gas

**4.** Read the sentence below. Choose the best word or phrase to complete the sentence.

> **it is available everywhere**
> **it never harms wildlife**
> **it will never run out**
> **it produces little or no pollution**

There are many benefits to using renewable energy sources. One of the benefits of using renewable energy sources is that _____ . Another

benefit is that _____ .

**5.** Read the sentence below. Choose the best word or phrase to complete the sentence.

> **heat**             **pollution**
>
> **harm wildlife**      **cause droughts**

One drawback of hydroelectric energy is that dams can _____ .

Geothermal energy comes from _____ . Solar energy does not result

in _____ .

**6.** Choose the correct answer. An electricity generating plant doesn't want to use biomass to produce electricity due its drawbacks. Which of these is a drawback of using biomass to produce electricity?

    **a.** It is nonrenewable.

    **b.** It is very costly to use.

    **c.** It can be used in few places.

    **d.** It can produce air pollution.

# Lesson Roundup

**A.** Choose the correct words to complete each sentence.

| | | | |
|---|---|---|---|
| coal | pollution | natural gas | biomass |
| oil | severe weather | radiation | |

One example of a renewable energy resource is _____. One drawback

of nonrenewable energy resources is that they produce _____.

**B.** Fill in the term of the renewable resource to the row that features the benefits and drawbacks.

| | | | | |
|---|---|---|---|---|
| hydroelectric | solar | biomass | wind | geothermal |

| Renewable Resource | Benefits | Drawbacks |
|---|---|---|
| | • renewable<br>• clean energy | • needs sun to work<br>• equipment is expensive |
| | • renewable<br>• clean energy | • long spinning blades can hurt birds<br>• turbines are loud<br>• large area of land is needed |
| | • renewable<br>• clean energy | • dams are expensive<br>• reservoirs flood valuable land<br>• dams can harm fish and other life by changing depth and temperature of rivers<br>• reservoirs take away wildlife habitat |
| | • renewable<br>• low pollution | • only available in certain areas<br>• some processes release water containing chemicals that can pollute the air |
| | • renewable<br>• less polluting than fossil fuels | • burning the material can produce air pollution |

**C.** What other information did you learn about the benefits or drawbacks of using renewable resources for energy?

_____

_____

# How Can People Reduce the Impact of Land-Based Hazards?

A picture of a volcanic eruption is amazing. You can see the hot lava and billowing ashes and gases the volcano releases. How can people stay safe when a volcanic eruption happens?

**By the end of this lesson . . .**
You'll be able to describe some natural hazards and tell how people can stay safe when they occur.

© Houghton Mifflin Harcourt • Image Credits: ©Westend61/Getty Images

# Can You Explain It?

▷ Explore Online

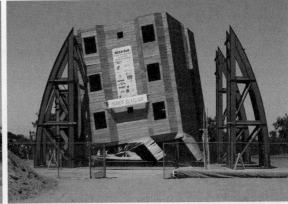

At the University of California, San Diego, engineers construct buildings to test their ability to withstand earthquakes. The buildings sit on a giant "shake table" that models how Earth moves during an earthquake.

**1.** In what ways can people reduce the impact of land-based natural hazards, such as earthquakes?

_____

_____

_____

_____

_____

_____

**Tip**

Learn more about ways that people can design solutions to problems in How Do Engineers Define Problems? and How Do Engineers Design Solutions?

 **EVIDENCE NOTEBOOK** Look for this icon to help you gather evidence to answer the question above.

# Land-Based Natural Hazards

## Our Active Earth

Earth has many processes that help shape its surface. But these can also cause natural hazards. A **natural hazard** is an Earth process that threatens people and property.

### Types of Land-Based Hazards

Use the images and captions to learn about land-based hazards.

When a volcano erupts, it can release lava, rocks, ash, and poisonous gases. These can be dangerous to people and surrounding property.

Landslides can be falling or flowing soil, mud, rocks, or snow. They can knock down trees and bury homes and other property.

In an earthquake, the ground shakes violently. This shaking can collapse buildings and bridges. Roads and walkways can crack and crumple.

During a wildfire, an area of forest, shrub, or grassland burns out of control. Buildings can be completely destroyed and people have to leave.

**2.** Why is it important for people to be warned about natural hazards?

_____

_____

_____

**HANDS-ON  Apply What You Know**

## Make Your Own Seismometer

**3.** A seismometer detects and measures ground movement. In this interaction you will make a seismometer.

**Materials**
- shoebox without lid
- ruler
- pointed-tip scissors
- construction paper
- clear adhesive tape
- 2 rubber bands
- fine line marker
- yarn or string

## Procedure:

**a.** Working in a team of two or three, use a ruler to measure a 10 cm cutting line along the bottom edge of each long side of the box.

**b.** Cut a slit along each cutting line.

**c.** Cut the paper into strips slightly less than 10 cm wide.

**d.** Attach the pieces together with clear adhesive tape to form one long strip.

**e.** Insert the strip of paper into the slits so the ends of the strip extend out of the slits.

**f.** Attach two rubber bands so the bands are stretched wide to the sides of the two box slits.

**g.** Cut two pieces of yarn or string and tie the marker into place between the rubber bands so the tip lightly rests on the strip of paper in the box.

**h.** Working together, one partner jiggles the box while the other pulls the paper through to get a continuous reading of the magnitude of the simulated earthquake.

**4.** Identify and describe a problem or difficulty you noticed while using the seismometer.

_____

_____

**5.** Describe one way your seismometer could be improved.

_____

_____

**6.** Think about your model and how it works. Which part(s) remain relatively stationary during an earthquake, and how does this make the seismometer work?

_____

_____

_____

**7.** What would an Earth scientist need to do to be able to interpret a seismometer such as yours? How would he or she "read" it?

_____

_____

# Cause and Effect

The cause of every natural hazard is related to an Earth process. The effects of these events can be very destructive.

## Causes and Effects of Land-Based Hazards

**8.** Read about each of the land-based hazards shown here. Then complete the table.

 Explore Online

Volcanic eruptions occur when melted rock bursts through an opening in Earth's crust. The hot lava can cause wildfires. Falling ash can cause landslides.

Sometimes enormous pieces of Earth's crust suddenly grind against each other, causing an earthquake. The ground shakes so hard that buildings can collapse.

Landslides can be triggered by volcanic eruptions, or earthquakes. Rock slides and snow avalanches occur on steep slopes, but mud can flow on even a gentle slope.

Wildfires are caused by human activities, volcanic eruptions, dry conditions, and lightning. They can destroy natural environments and homes, and also cause landslides.

| Natural hazard | Cause and effect |
|---|---|
| | Cause—Melted rock bursts through a crack in Earth's crust. |
| wildfire | Effect— |
| | Cause—Earth's enormous rock plates grind against each other. |
| landslide | Cause— |

## Do the Math
## Richter Scale

The Richter scale can be used to measure and compare strength of earthquakes. Each magnitude on the Richter scale is 10 times greater than the one before it. So a magnitude 3 earthquake is 10 times stronger than a magnitude 2 earthquake and 100 times stronger than a magnitude 1 earthquake.

| Magnitude | Ground shaking |
|-----------|----------------|
| 1–3 | not felt |
| 3–4 | weak |
| 4–5 | light/moderate |
| 5–6 | strong/very strong |
| 6–7 | very strong/severe |
| 7+ | severe/violent/extreme |

9. Use the table to determine the magnitude of an earthquake in which you felt the ground shake.

_____

_____

10. How much stronger is an earthquake that measures 7 on the Richter scale than an earthquake that measures 5 on the Richter scale?

   a. 2 times as strong

   b. 10 times stronger

   c. 100 times stronger

   d. 1,000 times stronger

11. If you use the number 1 to represent the strength of a magnitude 1 earthquake, explain what number would be used to represent the strength of a magnitude 5 earthquake.

_____

_____

## Language SmArts
## Drawing Examples from Text

12. Use examples from the text to explain why an understanding of the causes and effects of land-based hazards is important to helping people stay safe.

_____

_____

_____

**EVIDENCE NOTEBOOK**  In your Evidence Notebook, identify three specific facts about natural hazards that would be important to engineers who are designing ways to keep people safe. Explain why you included each fact.

# Hazards Here and There

Some natural hazards occur more frequently in some places than in others. Maps can be used to show this information.

## Earthquake Maps

These maps provide information about the number of earthquakes of magnitude 3.5 or greater in different states from 1974–2003. Use the information in the maps to answer the questions.

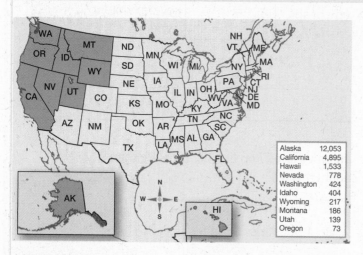

| Alaska | 12,053 |
| California | 4,895 |
| Hawaii | 1,533 |
| Nevada | 778 |
| Washington | 424 |
| Idaho | 404 |
| Wyoming | 217 |
| Montana | 186 |
| Utah | 139 |
| Oregon | 73 |

This map shows the ten states that experienced the greatest number of earthquakes.

**13.** Other than Alaska, how would you describe the location of the states in the "top ten" earthquake list?

_____

_____

| New Mexico | 38 |
| Arkansas | 34 |
| Arizona | 32 |
| Colorado | 24 |
| Tennessee | 22 |
| Missouri | 21 |
| Texas | 20 |
| Illinois | 17 |
| Oklahoma | 17 |
| Maine | 16 |

This map shows the states ranked 11 through 20 based on the number of earthquakes.

**14.** Which states in this list had more than one earthquake per year during the 29 years shown?

_____

_____

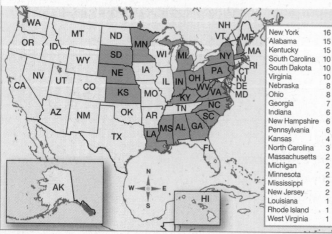

| New York | 16 |
| Alabama | 15 |
| Kentucky | 15 |
| South Carolina | 10 |
| South Dakota | 10 |
| Virginia | 10 |
| Nebraska | 8 |
| Ohio | 8 |
| Georgia | 7 |
| Indiana | 6 |
| New Hampshire | 6 |
| Pennsylvania | 6 |
| Kansas | 4 |
| North Carolina | 3 |
| Massachusetts | 2 |
| Michigan | 2 |
| Minnesota | 2 |
| Mississippi | 2 |
| New Jersey | 2 |
| Louisiana | 1 |
| Rhode Island | 1 |
| West Virginia | 1 |

This map shows all the remaining states that experienced at least one earthquake.

**15.** How does the location of the states shown here compare to the location of the states that had the most earthquakes?

_____

_____

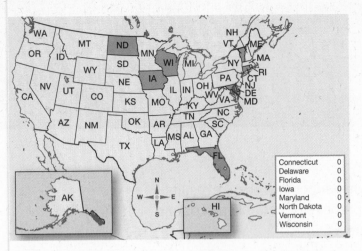

| Connecticut | 0 |
| Delaware | 0 |
| Florida | 0 |
| Iowa | 0 |
| Maryland | 0 |
| North Dakota | 0 |
| Vermont | 0 |
| Wisconsin | 0 |

This map shows which states did not experience an earthquake.

**16.** How would you describe the possibility of an earthquake in the states shown in this map?

_____

_____

_____

**17.** Locate your state on one of the maps. What can you infer about earthquakes in your state based on the information in the maps?

_____

_____

**18.** Using the maps, choose the state that makes each sentence most correct.

| Vermont | Minnesota | Illinois | New York |
|---------|-----------|----------|----------|
| North Carolina | California | Nebraska | New Mexico |

Among the states listed above , the most earthquakes happen in

_____. Of the states listed, the smallest number of earthquakes

happen in _____.

## Putting It Together

**19.** Choose the correct word to complete each sentence.

| landslides | earthquakes | volcanic eruptions | wildfires |

Two hazards caused by natural processes that occur under

Earth's surface are _____ and

_____. Processes occurring on

Earth's surface are the direct cause of _____ and

_____.

# Reducing the Impacts of Land-Based Hazards

## Expect the Unexpected

You can't prevent natural hazards from happening. They're results of Earth's processes. However, you can prepare for natural hazards and plan for how to be safe when they do occur.

### Preparation and Response

**20.** For each natural hazard shown, research to find out how to prepare ahead of time and respond while it is happening.

| Hazard | Preparation | Response |
|---|---|---|
| Volcanic eruption | | |
| Earthquake | | |
| Landslide | | |
| Wildfire | | |

**21.** Circle the pictures that represent a way to stay safe during an earthquake.

# Disaster Supply Kit

**22.** Select one type of natural hazard. Brainstorm and research what supplies would be important to include in a disaster supply kit for this type of hazard. Draw a diagram of your supply kit. Identify the type of hazard it is designed for. List the things you will include, and write an explanation of why each item is important.

**Engineer It!**
# Earthquake-Resistant Buildings

**23.** How would you design an earthquake-resistant building? When engineers design buildings to be resistant to earthquakes, they consider many factors. Look at the picture to learn more.

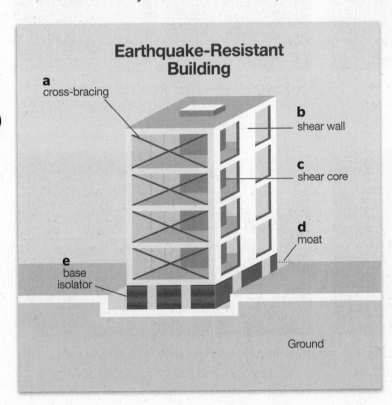

Earthquake-Resistant Building

a cross-bracing
b shear wall
c shear core
d moat
e base isolator
Ground

**a.** Cross-braces are diagonal. They help reinforce the building and increase its stability.

**b.** Shear walls are vertical walls. They help make the building solid and stiff. They increase the ability of the structure to withstand rocking.

**c.** In the middle of a building, you might find a shear core. This is an inside structure made out of shear walls. You might find a shear core around an elevator.

**d.** A moat is an area around the outside of a building. This helps keep the building from being damaged by nearby buildings that might not be earthquake resistant.

**e.** A base isolator separates the building from the ground. A base isolator is made to absorb the movement of the earthquake.

**24.** Describe two specific ways that engineers make buildings earthquake resistant.

![Engineer It icon]

# Engineer It!
# Reducing Impacts with Technology

Earth's natural processes create quite a few hazards. Humans cannot prevent earthquakes, volcanic eruptions, or other natural hazards. The good news is that technology can help us be safer from natural hazards.

**25.** Use the pictures and captions to identify the hazard for each technology in the first column. Then research other technology that helps keeps us safe. Write these in the third column labeled AdditionalTechnologies.

When melted rock moves upward, it tilts the ground around it. A tiltmeter records these changes, helping scientists predict eruptions.

Seismograph readings show the size and location of an earthquake's source, including how deep underground it is.

Firebreaks prevent wildfires from spreading. A firebreak is a strip of land that does not provide fuel for the fire, so the fire usually cannot move past it.

Piles and retaining walls are built to keep unstable rocks and soil from sliding down a hillside.

| Hazard | Technology | Additional Technologies |
|---|---|---|
|  | Firebreaks |  |
|  | Tiltmeter |  |
|  | Piles and retaining walls |  |
|  | Seismograph |  |

## Make a Plan

**26.** For every natural hazard, there are ways to plan ahead to be safer. With a team of three or four students, choose a land-based natural hazard. Using what you learn during your research, create a safety video about that hazard. Submit your video to your teacher.

**27. Language SmArts** For the natural hazard you chose above, make a plan for each member of your family should that hazard occur. Carry out research by integrating information from two texts, then write your plan below.

_____

_____

_____

_____

**28.** Volcanic eruption can cause other land-based hazards to occur. Identify one of these, and describe preparation for that hazard.

_____

_____

_____

_____

**29.** A safety warning on the evening news based on results of tiltmeter readings would indicate that a family needed to prepare for _____.

    **a.** a volcanic eruption

    **b.** an earthquake

    **c.** a storm

**EVIDENCE NOTEBOOK** Engineers are designing technology to keep people safe during an earthquake. How might seismographs and maps showing the history of earthquakes in an area help them? Write your answer in your Evidence Notebook.

# What's the Pattern?

Because we can't prevent natural hazards, it's important to have some idea about when they might happen so that people can get to safety or at least be prepared. Scientists try to know a hazard is coming by watching for patterns in nature that serve as warning signs.

## Patterns that Are Warning Signs

**30.** Use the pictures and captions to list warning signs for each hazard.

| Natural hazard | | | | |
|---|---|---|---|---|
| Warning signs | | | | |

Scientists can predict a volcanic eruption if they see a pattern of movement of the ground, earthquakes, and release of volcanic gases.

Earthquakes are more likely in areas that have had earthquakes in the past and have strain in Earth's crust. Earth movement and strain are measured using seismometers, creepmeters, strainmeters, tiltmeters, and lasers.

Landslides happen suddenly, with little warning, often triggered by earthquakes, volcanoes, heavy rains, and wildfires.

Under dry conditions, once a wildfire has started, satellites or aircraft can find it. Then people are alerted and take action.

**31.** Imagine that scientists are monitoring an area using a seismometer. They notice patterns of small movements of Earth's surface, and they know this is an area where there is strain in Earth's crust. Based on the patterns you know, which of these natural hazards could happen soon? Circle all that apply.

a. lava erupting from volcano      c. wildfire

b. landslide      d. earthquake

**32.** Individual landslides cannot be predicted, but scientists know occurrence of certain hazards can make a landslide more likely. Identify one of those hazards, and explain how it can trigger a landslide.

_____

_____

_____

**33.** What pattern of events is most likely to indicate that a wildfire might occur in an area?

a. low rainfall amounts

b. small movements of Earth's surface

c. change in the tilt of the land in an area

d. shifts in Earth materials on a hillside

**Language SmArts**
# Summarizing Information

**Tip**

The English Language Arts Handbook can provide help with understanding how to summarize information.

**34.** Choose the correct words to complete each sentence.

| watch | patterns | prevent | future | warning |

You cannot _____ natural hazards, but you can plan what you will do during one. Natural hazards can't be predicted far in advance, but studying _____ makes some advance warning possible.

Technology helps keep people safe by giving a _____ that a hazard has begun or by reducing the impact of the hazard in another way.

# Reduce the Risk

Landslides are land-based natural hazards that can damage property and injure people and animals. They occur when materials such as soil and rocks slide down a slope. Earthquakes and human activity can cause landslides. For example, building roads and homes can change the slope of an area.

**Scenario:** Imagine you have been hired by an engineering firm to develop a way to reduce the impact of landslides on a specific slope.

---

**Materials provided**
- large shallow container (painting tray or bin)
- mixture of soil, sand, gravel, and rocks
- toy cars and milk carton houses
- 1 liter of water
- newspapers
- 1-liter bottle with small holes on the bottom

**Materials from your budget**
- 5 units per craft stick
- 5 units per "tree" (twigs)
- 5 units per of piece of cardboard
- 5 units per medium rock
- 5 units per piece of netting
- 1 unit per wire twist tie

---

## Objective

**Collaborate** with a group to develop a plan to reduce the impact of a landslide.

**Find a Problem:** What question will you investigate to meet this objective?

_____

_____

## Procedure

**STEP 1  Brainstorm:** Discuss criteria for a successful design to reduce the impact of a landslide. Consider constraints on your design.

| Criteria | Constraints |
|---|---|
| ☐ Reduces the amount of materials that moves to the bottom of the slope | ☐ Uses available material |
| ☐ Reduces damage to houses and or cars | ☐ Stays within a budget of 100 units |
|  | ☐ Stays within the alloted time set by the teacher |

**STEP 2** **Research** landslides and methods used to reduce their impact, such as retaining walls, piles, and buttress walls. Brainstorm ideas for designs that could reduce the impact of a landslide. Record at least three ideas here.

_____

_____

_____

_____

_____

**STEP 3** Build a hillside of earth materials in the bin or tray. Build houses or a road with cars at the bottom of the slope. Simulate a landslide with your water bottle by sprinkling a liter of water over your hillside. Carefully observe and record the impact of the landslide. Describe the amount of earth materials that move down the slope and the impact on the cars or houses.

_____

_____

_____

**STEP 4** **Plan:** Review the materials available for your design and their "costs." Review the budget of 100 units. Choose one design to develop as a prototype. Identify the design chosen to develop, and explain why your group chose this design.

_____

_____

_____

_____

**STEP 5** Use the space below to draw a model of your design.

[blank box]

**STEP 6 Build:** Using your group's model and your available budget, build a design solution for reducing the impact of landslides. Describe any modifications you needed to make as you built your design solution.

_____

_____

_____

_____

**STEP 7 Test:** Carry out a test of your design by simulating conditions that could start a landslide. Record the results of your test here. Be sure to describe any damage to the houses or cars.

_____

_____

_____

_____

**STEP 8  Evaluate and Redesign:** Explain how you will modify your design based on the results of your test. You will need to stay within your budget.

_____

_____

_____

_____

_____

**STEP 9**  Modify your design, and make any necessary improvements. Keep in mind, you will need to stay within your budget. The slope, road, and houses need to be placed the same in all trials. Test your modified prototype. Describe what happened.

_____

_____

_____

_____

_____

**STEP 10  Communicate:** In the space below, write a summary to communicate the details of your final design.

_____

_____

_____

_____

_____

_____

## Analyze Results

**STEP 11** Compare your team's results with those of a different team. Describe how and why your results were similar to or different from the other team's results.

_____

_____

_____

**STEP 12** What method did you use to determine whether your design reduced the impact of a landslide?

_____

_____

_____

_____

**STEP 13** Describe a specific aspect of your design that helped reduce the impact of a landslide.

_____

_____

_____

_____

## Draw Conclusions

**STEP 14** Make a claim about the success of your design. Cite evidence to support your claim.

_____

_____

**STEP 15** What other questions do you have about ways that engineers can design devices to reduce the impact of landslides?

_____

_____

_____

# Discover More

**Check out this path . . . or go online to choose one of these other paths.**

**People in Science & Engineering**

- Hawaii Island Lava Hazard Zone Maps
- Debate About A Volcano Solution

## Dr. Lucy Jones

Dr. Lucy Jones was world famous as a seismologist, an earthquake scientist. She was an expert at understanding, predicting, and preparing for earthquakes.

Dr. Jones studied small earthquakes that are sometimes followed by a bigger, more damaging one. Dr. Jones developed a way to predict how likely it is that a small earthquake will be followed by a bigger one.

Lucy Jones did even more. She worked to improve how we prepare for natural hazards. She recommended that people keep fire extinguishers in their homes and know how to use them. She believesd that homes in areas of high earthquake risk could be fixed in important small ways to make them safer.

Dr. Lucy Jones at work.

**35.** Which of the following is not a job of Dr. Lucy Jones?

- **a.** understanding earthquakes
- **b** stopping earthquakes
- **c.** predicting earthquakes
- **d.** preparing for earthquakes

**36.** Go online to the U.S. Geological Survey website, and gather data about earthquakes of magnitude 2.5 or greater in the past year. Determine the five states that had the most earthquakes, and list the states and the number of earthquakes in the table.

| State | Frequency |
|-------|-----------|
|       |           |
|       |           |
|       |           |
|       |           |
|       |           |

**37.** Use the information from the U.S. Geological Survey to plot the location of the five most recent earthquakes in the United States on the map.

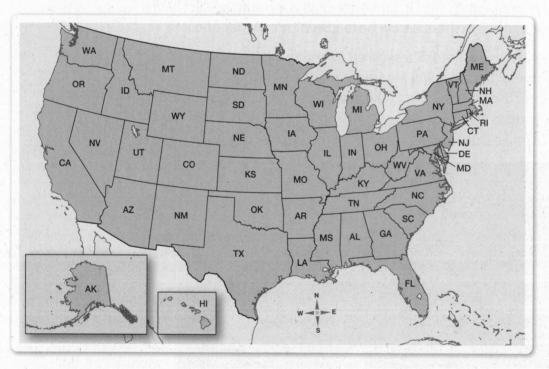

**38.** Compare your data to the data found on the earthquake frequency map shown earlier in the lesson. Explain how your results are similar to or different from the information shown in those maps.

_____

_____

_____

# Lesson Check

Name _____

## Can You Explain It?

 Explore Online

1. What are some ways people can reduce the impact of land-based natural hazards such as earthquakes? Be sure to do the following:

   • Describe several land-based natural hazards.

   • Describe ways that the impact of natural hazards can be lessened.

   • Explain how engineering processes can reduce the impact of natural hazards.

   • In particular, describe how the impacts of earthquakes could be reduced.

📋 **EVIDENCE NOTEBOOK** Use the information you've collected in your Evidence Notebook to help you cover each point.

_____

_____

_____

_____

_____

_____

_____

_____

_____

## Checkpoints

2. Which of these is a sign that a volcano will probably erupt soon? Circle all that apply.

   **a.** ground movement          **c.** earthquakes

   **b.** increasing landslides     **d.** changes in volcanic gases

**3.** Draw lines to match each word with the correct picture of a technology that can reduce the impact of that type of hazard.

**Natural Hazards**

volcanic eruption

wildfire

earthquake

landslide

**4.** The risk of which land-based natural hazard is increased during time periods when there is not much rain?

   **a.** volcanic eruption          **c.** earthquake

   **b.** landslide                          **d.** wildfire

**5.** Use the word bank to write the most likely cause of each of these effects.

   | earthquake          volcano |

   **a.** landslide _____

   **b.** crumpled roads _____

   **c.** building collapse _____

   **d.** release of poisonous gases _____

**6.** Which natural hazards are most likely to be the direct cause of a wildfire? Circle all that apply.

   **a.** earthquake

   **b.** volcano

   **c.** landslide

   **d.** lightning strike

# Lesson Roundup

**A.** Choose the correct words to complete each sentence.

When melted rock and gases burst through an opening in Earth's

crust, a(n) _____ occurs. Sudden movement of the

rocky plates that form Earth's crust result in a(n) _____.

A(n) _____ happens when materials slide down a slope.

What else have you learned about natural hazards in this lesson?

_____

_____

_____

| volcanic eruption |
| earthquake |
| landslide |
| wildfire |

**B.** Choose a technology from the word bank that can lessen the impact of each natural hazard.

| earthquake resistant building  firebreak  retaining wall  tiltmeter |

 _____

 _____

 _____

 _____

What else have you learned about natural hazard safety in this lesson?

_____

_____

_____

# How Can People Reduce the Impact of Water-Based Hazards

The land in this picture is dry and cracked. Many plants probably cannot grow here. What causes conditions like this? And how does it impact people?

_____

**By the end of this lesson . . .**
you'll be able to describe some water-based hazards and tell how people can stay safe when they occur.

© Houghton Mifflin Harcourt • Image Credits: ©Jyesheen Chenglstock

# Can You Explain It?

These people are placing bags full of sand along a river. They know that lots of rain is expected, and the river might overflow its banks.

**1.** How will these actions help reduce the impact of a water-based hazard? What else could reduce the impact of this hazard?

_____

_____

_____

_____

_____

_____

_____

© Houghton Mifflin Harcourt • Image Credits: ©Keith Douglas/Alamy

**Tip**

Learn more about the affects of water on Earth's surface in *How Does Water Shape Earth's Surface?*

 **EVIDENCE NOTEBOOK** Look for this icon to help you gather evidence to answer the questions above.

# Water-Based Natural Hazards

## Water, Water, Everywhere

Some of the natural processes of Earth's surface, its oceans, and its atmosphere can produce water-based hazards. Deep below Earth's surface, pieces of the crust can suddenly move, producing waves that are unusually large and dangerous. Above Earth's surface, great storms can produce heavy rain and wind so strong that it destroys buildings.

### Types of Water-Based Hazards

Use the images and captions to learn about some kinds of water-based hazards.

 A hurricane is a strong storm with devastating winds and heavy rains. It is not safe to be outdoors during a hurricane.

 A tsunami is a powerful type of wave. It rushes onto the ocean shore like a high flood. It can have enough force to smash buildings.

 During a drought, there is much less water than usual. People and animals struggle to have enough water.

 During a flood, water covers the land and may flood homes as well. Floodwater can ruin property and threaten people's safety.

**2.** What are some impacts of water-based hazards?

_____

_____

_____

_____

**3.** Which water-based hazard's impacts are caused by a lack of water?

   **a.** hurricane       **c.** drought

   **b.** tsunami        **d.** flood

# Do the Math
# Classifying Hurricanes

Wind speeds are used to assign hurricanes to categories. Category 1 storms have the lowest wind speeds. Category 5 storms have the highest wind speeds. Scientists can use these classifications to compare hurricanes and tell people the strength of the hurricane they have to prepare for.

| Category | Sustained Winds (km/hr) | Sustained Winds (mph) |
|---|---|---|
| 1 | 119 to 153 km/hr | 74-95 mph |
| 2 | 154 to 177 km/hr | 96-110 mph |
| 3 | 178 to 208 km/hr | 111-129 mph |
| 4 | 209 to 251 km/hr | 130-156 mph |
| 5 | 252 km/hr and greater | 157 mph or higher |

| 2015 Atlantic Hurricanes | | |
|---|---|---|
| Hurricane | Maximum Sustained Winds (km/hr) | Maximum Sustained Winds (mph) |
| Danny | 185 km/hr | 115mph |
| Fred | 140 km/hr | 85 mph |
| Joaquin | 250 km/hr | 155mph |
| Kate | 120 km/hr | 75 mph |

4. Complete the sentence and expression for each hurricane. The first one has been completed as an example.

   **A.** Hurricane Danny is a Category _____3_____ hurricane because its winds were greater than ____178 km/hr____ but less than ____208 km/hr____.

   **B.** Hurricane Fred is a Category _____ hurricane because its winds were greater than _____ but less than _____.

   **C.** Hurricane Joaquin is a Category _____ hurricane because its winds were greater than _____ but less than _____.

5. Forecasters predict the strength of hurricanes so people can prepare for them. What category is Hurricane Kate and how would knowing that help someone prepare?

   _____

   _____

   _____

# Connecting Cause and Effect

Hazards have causes and effects. If people know the causes of a hazard, it can help them make predictions. If they know the effects of a hazard, it can help them prepare.

## Causes and Effects of Water-Based Hazards

**6.** Read about each of the water-based hazards shown here. Then complete the table.

 Explore Online

A hurricane forms as the energy in warm ocean water fuels strong winds and heavy rains. It causes storm surges, flooding, landslides, and wind damage.

Droughts are caused by long dry periods. Droughts can last years. A drought's effects are related to a lack of water. Dried up plants burn easily, so droughts can lead to wildfires.

Tsunamis are a series of giant waves, caused by undersea earthquakes, landslides, or volcanic eruptions. Tsunamis move onto shore, washing away almost anything in their path.

River flooding is caused by heavy rain or snow melt. Coastal flooding is caused by storm surges. Floodwater can damage structures and cause landslides.

| Natural hazard | Cause and effect |
|---|---|
| hurricane | Effect— |
|  | Cause—Heavy rainfall, melting snow, or a storm surge raises the water level. |
| tsunami | Effect— |
|  | Effect—Plants, animals, and people do not have enough water, and the wildfire danger is high. |

## Take Action

7. Imagine you and your family live in a region called Watertown. Your region is currently being impacted by a drought. Carry out one activity from the list below to show your understanding of the impact of a drought and how the effects of a drought can be lessened.

- Create a poster informing the residents of Watertown what they can do to help reduce the impacts of a drought. You will need to identify two specific impacts of the drought, and tell how the effects of those two impacts could be decreased.

- Write a letter to the editor of *Watertown Newspaper* that draws attention to the need for residents to take actions to reduce the impact of a drought. Include evidence to support your claim.

- In a group, role play a meeting of interested community members about what action can be taken to offset the impact of the drought that has hit the Watertown region. Assume specific roles, such as farmer, truck driver, and mayor. Each person should present information specific to his or her assigned roles.

- In a group, brainstorm and come up with ways you can help members of Watertown save water in their house, in their backyard, and at their school. Present your ideas in the form of a three-column table.

8. What information about the causes and effects of drought did you apply to complete the activity you chose?

_____

_____

_____

**EVIDENCE NOTEBOOK** In your Evidence Notebook, identify how information about the causes and effects of water-based hazards can be used to lessen their impacts.

# Where Are There Droughts?

Some water-based hazards, such as droughts, occur more frequently in some places than in others. Drought monitor maps can be used to show this information.

## Drought Maps

The maps provide information about areas experiencing drought. Use the information in the maps to answer the questions.

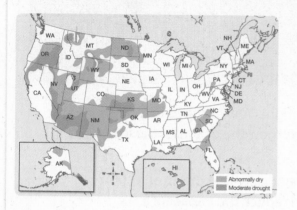

The areas shown on this map are experiencing abnormally dry conditions to moderate drought conditions. This level of drought has some effect on crops, and water-use restrictions are voluntary, not required.

**9.** What conditions could cause these areas to change classification to severe drought?

_____

_____

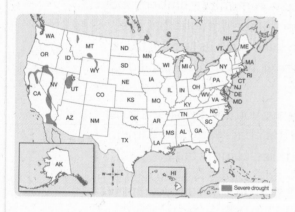

The areas shown on this map are experiencing severe drought conditions. In these areas, crops are strongly affected and water-use restrictions and water shortages are common.

**10.** How does the size of the area experiencing severe drought compare to the size of the area experiencing abnormally dry or moderate drought conditions?

_____

_____

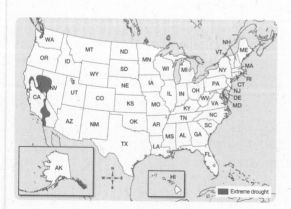

The areas shown on this map are experiencing extreme drought conditions. These areas experience substantial crop losses and extreme water shortages.

**11.** In which geographic portion of the United States are there extreme drought conditions?

_____

_____

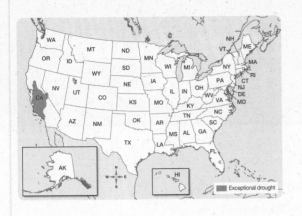

The areas shown on this map are experiencing exceptional drought conditions. Drought of this level results in widespread crop loss and reduced water levels in streams, lakes, and reservoirs.

**12.** What is one way that exceptional drought conditions in part of the United States could affect other parts of the country?

_____

_____

_____

**13.** Locate your state on one of the drought monitor maps. What drought conditions, if any, are being experienced in your state?

_____

_____

**14.** Using the drought monitor maps, choose the state that makes each sentence most correct.

| | | | |
|---|---|---|---|
| **Pennsylvania** | **Ohio** | **Illinois** | **New York** |
| **North Carolina** | **California** | **Kansas** | |

There are exceptional drought conditions in _____.

There are abnormally dry and moderate drought conditions but no

exceptional drought conditions in _____.

---

**Language SmArts**

# Analyze and Evaluate Internet Information

**15.** What are some ways that people can apply information about water-based natural hazards to help them stay safe?

_____

_____

_____

_____

© Houghton Mifflin Harcourt

**Tip**

The English Language Arts Handbook can provide help with understanding how to analyze and evaluate Internet information.

# Reducing the Impacts of Water-Based Hazards

## Think Ahead!

Most water-based hazards cannot be prevented. That's why it's important to know how to prepare for and respond to a variety of hazards.

### Staying Safe

**16.** For each natural hazard shown in the chart, research to find out how to prepare ahead of time and how to respond while it is happening.

| Hazard | Preparation | Response |
|---|---|---|
| Hurricane | | |
| Tsunami | | |
| Flood | | |
| Drought | | |

**17.** Select which pictures represent a way to stay safe during a hurricane. Circle all the pictures that apply.

© Houghton Mifflin Harcourt

Water from a powerful tsunami can travel as far as 16 km inland if the shoreline is not elevated much above sea level. A tsumani can devastate the area. Learn more about tsunamis.

A tsunami begins with an underwater disturbance, such as an earthquake.

When the first wave reaches shallow water, it slows down. Its height increases.

A tsunami harms people and property by both the force of its impact and the amount of water it moves onto land.

After the water has drained away, many people find their homes, schools, and businesses are destroyed.

After a tsunami, people need to clean up and rebuild.

**18.** Natural hazards, such as tsunamis, are triggered by Earth processes. They can harm many people, homes, and property, as well as animals and their habitats. What is one way people can reduce the impact of a tsunami?

_____

_____

# Engineer It!
# Using Technology to Reduce Impacts

Geostationary operational environmental satellites (GOES) move so that they hover above the same place on Earth. Information collected helps predict hurricanes and other severe weather events. They are used to warn people about hurricanes, tornadoes, and flash floods and can help reduce the impact of a drought.

Deep-ocean tsunami detection buoys measure the height of the water's surface. If a tsunami wave passes under a buoy, the buoy transmits that information to the tsunami warning center via satellite. The network of buoys can help scientists predict when tsunami waves might reach shore.

A levee is like a wall alongside a river or other waterway to help keep floodwater from spilling onto nearby land. Levees are usually made of packed dirt. Sandbags can be stacked to build walls that are similar to levees.

Reservoirs are usually constructed by building a dam on a river. Water collects in the reservoir, making it available during drier times. Sometimes, plastic balls are put over the reservoir to prevent evaporation. They also protect the water from dust, rain, chemicals and wildlife.

19. Identify the hazard for each technology in the first column. Then research other technology that helps keep us safe. Write these in the third column labeled "Additional technologies."

| hurricane | flood | tsunami | drought |

| Technology | Hazard | Additional technologies |
| --- | --- | --- |
| reservoirs | | |
| deep-ocean buoys | | |
| levees and sandbags | | |
| geostationary operational environmental satellites | | |

20. **Language SmArts** Choose a water-based natural hazard that occurs in your state, and describe a family emergency plan that would help keep you safe if you got a warning the hazard might occur. Carry out research if necessary to write your answer.

_____

_____

_____

_____

21. How do reservoirs reduce the impact of a drought?

_____

_____

22. Choose the correct response. A geostationary operational environmental satellite can _____.

   **a.** prevent a tsunami            **c.** prevent a flood

   **b.** reduce the impact of a        **d.** reduce the impact of a
       drought                              hurricane

### Engineer It!
# Improving Levees

Engineers inspect, maintain, and improve levees. Here are some examples of ways in which engineers reduce the impact of floods.

## Problem: Seepage

When water flows under or through a levee, it is called *seepage.* Engineers use several solutions to prevent seepage.

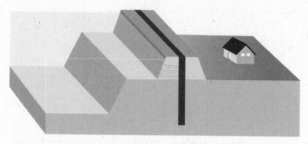

Seepage Cutoff Wall

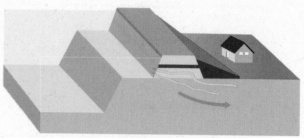

Seepage Berm

**Solution:** A seepage cutoff wall is an effective solution to seepage, but this solution cannot be used in all places.

**Solution:** Seepage berms are also used as a solution to seepage.

## Problem: Erosion

Levees are used to contain flowing water, so erosion of levees is a major problem.

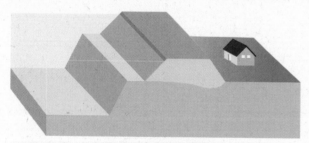

Widening and Flattening Slopes

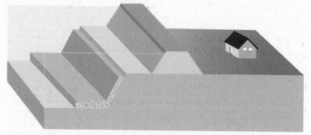

Rock Layer

**Solution:** One solution to erosion is widening and flattening the slope of the levee walls.

**Solution:** Adding a layer of rock over the levee materials is also a solution to the problem of erosion.

23. You are an engineer and have been contacted to design an alternative solution to the erosion of levees. What materials would you use? Describe what your solution would look like and how it would improve levees.

_____

_____

_____

## Problem: Water Flows Over Levee

Sometimes water flows over the top of levees that have been built.

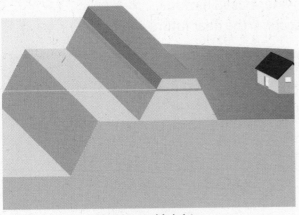

Increase Height

**Solution:** One solution for water that flows over a levee is to increase the height of the levee. That can lead to other problems, however, such as increased erosion.

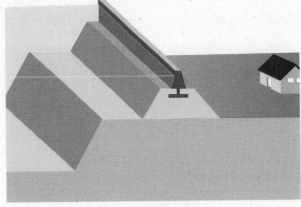

Flood Wall

**Solution:** Flood walls are made of concrete instead of clay, soil, and rock. They can be taller than many levees, so a flood wall can be a solution to water flowing over a levee.

**24.** Which best describes how flood walls and seepage cutoff walls are similar? Choose the correct response.

**a.** Both prevent water from moving.

**c.** Both prevent erosion that can occur on levees.

**b.** Both prevent water from moving under and through a levee.

**d.** Both are designed solutions to problems with levees.

**25.** How do well-maintained levees help reduce the impact of a water-based natural hazard?

_____

_____

_____

 **EVIDENCE NOTEBOOK** In your Evidence Notebook, describe a variety of methods that can be used to reduce the impact of flooding.

# Hazards and Patterns

Advance preparation can reduce the impact of water-based hazards. By identifying patterns of events that lead up to water-based hazards, scientists can warn people that a hazard might occur in the near future.

## Identifying Warning Signs

**26.** Use the pictures and captions to list warning signs for each hazard.

| Natural hazard | tsunami | flood | hurricane | drought |
|---|---|---|---|---|
| Warning signs | | | | |

Earthquakes may cause Tsunamis. If an earthquake moves a large volume of water above it, a tsunami could form. It might also travel thousands of kilometers across the ocean and cause devastation on distant shores. A noticeable fall or rise in the water level is another warning sign. An international warning system tells other countries whether their coasts are in danger.

Common warning signs for floods are intense rainfall, levee or dam failure, and even early snow melt. Flood warnings are given based on past patterns of flooding, readings from sensors placed in rivers, and information from weather satellites.

Until a hurricane has gotten close to making landfall, hurricane warning signs are not clearly visible. Some warning signs include an increase in ocean swell, wave frequency, wind speed, and rainfall. Scientists can track hurricanes using satellites and radar. This helps them warn people in areas that might be damaged.

Information about weather and climate patterns can be used to determine what areas might be at risk for droughts. Droughts happen when surface or underground water is greatly reduced. Knowing if a drought will affect an area is dependent on weather conditions, such as rainfall and temperature.

**27.** Circle the correct answer. Information about patterns in the location and intensity of earthquakes is most useful in helping people prepare for _____.

a. droughts

b. river flooding

c. hurricanes

d. tsunamis

## Putting It Together

**28.** Choose the correct words to complete each sentence. Use each word only once. Not all words will be used.

| patterns | flooding | future |
|----------|----------|--------|
| drought | tsunamis | warning |

Technology and information about _____ in nature can be used to help lessen the impact of water-based hazards. For example, levees can be used to lessen the impact of _____, and data about weather patterns can be used to predict areas where a _____ is possible.

## HANDS-ON ACTIVITY
# Is It Safe?

**Scenario:** Imagine a company called Wave Good-bye has hired you to build a small family neighborhood in a town on the seacoast. Part of your job is to make this small neighborhood as safe as possible from tsunami damage.

## Objective

**Collaborate** with your team to figure out how to reduce the damage a tsunami might do to a small neighborhood. Identify a solution to help reduce the impact. Use materials to design and build a model of your solutions. You have a budget of 500 units in local currency to build this small neighborhood.

**Find a Problem:** What question will you investigate to meet this objective?

_____

_____

_____

| Materials provided by "nature" | Materials from your budget |
|---|---|
| • large shallow container (tub or pan)<br>• water<br>• stiff, flat piece of cardboard to make waves | • 0 units per milk carton (house)<br>• 25 units per tree or plant<br>• 25 units per cup of gravel<br>• 10 units per newspaper page (land, when wadded into a ball)<br>• 10 units per cup of dirt<br>• 5 units per medium rock<br>• 5 units per cup of sand<br>• 5 units per craft stick |

## Procedure

**STEP 1 Brainstorm:** Discuss criteria for a successful design to reduce the impact of a tsunami. Consider constraints on your design. Write your ideas below.

_____

_____

| Criteria | Constraints |
|---|---|
| ☐ Reduce the damage done by the tsunami<br>☐ Reduce damage to houses | ☐ Use available material<br>☐ Stay within the budget<br>☐ Stay within the alloted time set by your teacher |

**STEP 2  Research:** Research tsunamis and methods used to reduce their impact. Brainstorm ideas for designs that could reduce the impact of a tsunami.

List and describe some of your ideas.

_____

_____

_____

**STEP 3  Plan:** Choose one design to develop as a prototype. Sketch it on a separate sheet of paper. Remember to keep the budget in mind.

Identify the design chosen and explain why your group chose it.

_____

_____

_____

**STEP 4  Build:** Make your model. Scrunch up newspaper and use it to make land on one half of the container. Flatten mud onto the newspaper, covering the land and sloping down to the sea. Add the features you have planned, including houses. Pour water into the empty side of the container.

**STEP 5  Test:** Test your prototype. Thrust a piece of cardboard through the water with a rapid force to make a wave. Repeat two additional times. After your test, identify and make any needed improvements in your design. Keep the budget in mind. You must keep the same amount of houses in the same location.  You will be re-testing your prototype in step 6.

What did you observe from your test? What improvements did you make in your design?

_____

_____

**STEP 6** Now that you have redesigned your prototype, test it again following the same steps.

Record your observations. How do your results compare to the results from your first prototype?

_____

_____

## Analyze Your Results

**STEP 7 Communicate:** Compare your team's results with those of a different team. Describe how and why your results were similar to or different from the other team's results.

_____

_____

**STEP 8 Evaluate and Redesign** Based on your two prototype designs, how could you improve your design further?

_____

_____

**STEP 9** What method did you use to determine whether your design reduced the impact of the tsunami?

_____

_____

## Draw Conclusions

**STEP 10** Make a claim about the success of your design? Cite evidence to support your claim.

_____

_____

_____

**STEP 11** What other questions do you have about ways that engineers can design devices to reduce the impact of tsunamis?

_____

_____

# Discover More

**Check out this path . . . or go online to choose one of these other paths.**

**Hurricanes and Their Effects**

- **Careers in Engineering**
- **Make It Safer**

Hurricanes form in warm ocean waters. When the moist air above the sea surface reaches 28 °C, it rises toward the cooler air above. When conditions are right, the moving air develops into a thunderstorm with strong winds and heavy rains. The storm gets larger as more warm, moist air rises up. The clouds begin moving in a circular pattern. The winds increase as the storm turns into a hurricane. Hurricanes cause flooding and heavy rains, which damage property and loosen soil and rocks, which can trigger landslides.

▶ **Explore Online**

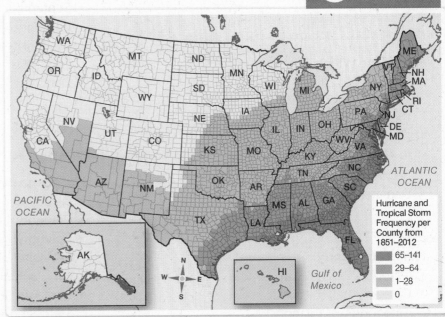

Hurricane and Tropical Storm frequency map

**29.** How could knowing where hurricanes and storms appear help you reduce the effects of hazardous weather? Use the map to your right and what you have read to support your answer.

_____

_____

**30.** What conclusions can you draw from the Hurricane and Tropical Storm frequency map?

_____

_____

The timeline shows seven different hurricanes that have occurred in this century.

Hurricanes can have a large impact.

**2004**

### Hurricane Charley
- August 13, 2004
- Category 4 at landfall
- Landfall along west coast of Florida
- Damage: $11 billion

**2004**

### Hurricane Frances
- September 5–6, 2004
- Category 2 at landfall
- Landfall near Stuart, Florida
- Damage: $9 billion

**2005**

### Hurricane Katrina
- August 29, 2005
- Category 1 at $1^{st}$ landfall, Category 3 at $2^{nd}$ landfall
- First landfall near Miami, Florida Second landfall near Buras, Louisiana
- Damage: $100+ billion

**2005**

### Hurricane Rita
- September 24, 2005
- Category 3 at landfall
- Landfall near Johnson's Bayou, Louisiana
- Damage: $10 billion

**2005**

### Hurricane Wilma
- October 24, 2005
- Category 5 at $1^{st}$ landfall, Category 3 at $2^{nd}$ landfall
- First landfall near Mexican Yucatan Peninsula Second landfall near Naples, Florida
- Damage: $21 billion

**2008**

### Hurricane Ike
- September 1–14, 2008
- Category 4 at first landfall
- Category 2 at final landfall
- First landfall in Cuba
- Final landall in Galveston Island, Texas
- Damages: 29.5 billion in the United States and $7.3 billion in Cuba

**2012**

### Hurricane Sandy
- October 22–29, 2012
- Category 1 at $1^{st}$ landfall Category 3 at $2^{nd}$ landfall
- First landfall in Jamaica Second landfall in Cuba Final landfall in Brigantine, New Jersey
- Damage: $62 billion in the United States and at least $315 million in the Caribbean

31. Use the information in the timeline to make a bar graph on a separate sheet of paper. Number the *y*-axis 1 through 5 and label it *Category*. Make a labeled bar for each hurricane to show the category at landfall. Make a bar for each landfall. Analyze your graph to see whether you notice any relationship between a hurricane's category and the amount of damage it caused. Submit your bar graph to your teacher.

# Lesson Check

Name _____

## Can You Explain It?

1. Look back at the image at the beginning of the lesson. What are some ways people can reduce the impact of a flood? Be sure to do the following:

   • Describe several water-based natural hazards that can affect humans.

   • Describe ways that the impact of water-based natural hazards, such as floods, can be lessened and people in a community can prepare for them.

   • Explain how testing, improving, and retesting design solutions can lead to ways that will help reduce the impact of water-based natural hazards.

   **EVIDENCE NOTEBOOK** Use the information you've collected in your Evidence Notebook to help you cover each point.

_____

_____

_____

_____

_____

_____

_____

_____

## Checkpoints

2. Choose the correct response. Which of these would show you whether your state is experiencing drought conditions?

   **a.** daily weather report          **c.** drought monitor map

   **b.** road map                      **d.** deep ocean buoy

**3.** Draw lines to match each word with the correct picture of a technology that can reduce the impact of that type of hazard.

**Natural Hazard**

hurricane

flood

tsunami

drought

**4.** The risk of which water-based natural hazard is increased during time periods when there is NOT much rain?
- **a.** tsunami
- **b.** flood
- **c.** drought
- **d.** hurricane

**5.** Complete the table by writing the hazard from the word bank in the box with its possible warning signs.

| A pattern of very dry weather | An earthquake under the ocean |
|---|---|
| A storm starting to develop over warm ocean water | A pattern of rapid temperature increase leading to snow melt near a river |

drought

tsunami

flood

hurricane

**6.** Which of these form in or over the ocean before causing damage on land? Select all that apply.
- **a.** tsunami
- **b.** flood
- **c.** drought
- **d.** hurricane

# Lesson Roundup

**A.** Choose the correct words to complete each sentence.

Weather conditions over warm ocean water can cause a

_____ to form, which can lead to a _____

near the coast. A _____ is a natural hazard that can lead

to water-use restrictions being put in place to conserve water.

| drought |
| tsunami |
| flood |
| hurricane |

What else have you learned about water-based natural hazards
in this lesson?

_____

_____

_____

**B.** For each water-based natural hazard shown here, identify a
technology and how it can lessen its impact.

_____

_____

_____

_____

_____

_____

_____

_____

# Avoiding Disaster

You are a small-town mayor in the midwestern United States. Last summer, your town experienced record rainfall and flooded for the first time in history. Nobody was hurt, but there was a lot of damage. This year, you and a group of volunteers are tasked with planning strategies to minimize the danger and damage of flooding.

It is your job as mayor to keep this from happening again.

**DEFINE YOUR TASK:** How will you know if your project is successful?

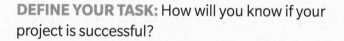

Before beginning, review the checklist at the end of this Unit Performance Task. Keep those items in mind as you proceed.

**RESEARCH:** Use online or library resources to learn about flood prevention methods. A good place to start is the Federal Emergency Management Agency (FEMA) website (http://www.fema.gov/). Find out how other communities have successfully prevented flooding. Note which methods seem the best. Cite your sources.

**BRAINSTORM:** Brainstorm three or more flood strategy ideas with your volunteers. Use what you have learned about natural hazards to identify what your strategy must achieve to be effective.

**PLAN YOUR PROCEDURE:** Consider the questions below as your group plans its flood strategy. Be sure to address the resources you will need and your overall goals and limits. Write a few sentences below to briefly summarize your strategy.

1. What kind of flood-control structures should we build, and where should we build them?
2. What other precautions should we take now?
3. How can we know if a flood threat is near?
4. What plan should be in place to react to a flood threat?
5. How can we educate the community about our plans?
6. How can we alert the community in the event of a threat?
7. What is our budget?
8. Will we need to raise more money, and if so, how and how much?

_____

_____

_____

**REPORT:** Create a document that details your flood strategy. Describe the precautions to be put in place. List steps to be carried out during a flood emergency. Be specific and complete.

**COMMUNICATE:** Present your flood plan to your class orally and with multimedia. Explain the reasoning behind your plan and discuss possible ways to revise and improve it.

## ☑ Checklist

**Review your project and check off each completed item.**

_____ Includes a statement defining your group's task.

_____ Includes research into and consideration of various flood-control strategies with sources cited.

_____ Includes a list of flood-plan precautions to be taken.

_____ Includes a description of flood-control structures with a list of materials needed to build them.

_____ Includes a plan of action to be followed during a flood.

_____ Includes an explanation of how the flood plan will be paid for.

_____ Includes an oral presentation with multimedia support.

# Unit Review

1. Which fuel source is made entirely of long-dead plants? Circle the correct choice.

   a. oil

   b. coal

   c. uranium

   d. natural gas

2. Which of the following is true of the product sold here? Circle all that apply.

   a. It is a natural resource.

   b. Its use creates pollution.

   c. It is a renewable resource.

   d. It is a nonrenewable resource.

3. Use the word bank to complete the sentences.

   | Oil | Uranium | Coal | Natural gas |

   _____ and oil are the remains of once-living

   organisms that died millions of years ago.

   _____ does not come from once-living material.

4. Indicate whether each type of energy is nonrenewable and causes pollution (NP) or renewable and nonpolluting (RN).

   Coal _____

   Wind _____

   Solar _____

   Water _____

   Natural gas _____

**5.** Use the word bank to complete the sentences.

| stored | created | reduced | increased |
|--------|---------|---------|-----------|

Energy from this source can be _____ for times when it is not being produced.

**6.** The methods used to generate electricity from both wind and water are similar. Explain how they are alike.

_____

_____

_____

_____

_____

_____

_____

**7.** Which of these are known to trigger tsunamis? Circle all that apply.

**a.** wildfires

**b.** landslides

**c.** volcanoes

**d.** hurricanes

**e.** earthquakes

**8.** What long-term natural disaster is pictured here?

Circle the correct choice.

**a.** a flood

**b.** a drought

**c.** a tsunami

**d.** a hurricane

**9.** Use the word bank to complete the sentences.

| | | |
|---|---|---|
| **hurricanes** | **half as strong as** | **twice as strong as** |
| **earthquakes** | **volcanoes** | **ten times stronger than** |

The Richter scale is used to measure the strength of _____.

Each level of the Richter scale is _____ the

previous level.

**10.** Air and water at different temperatures can produce violent storms such as hurricanes. Explain how temperature, water, and air are related to a hurricane.

_____

_____

_____

_____

# Interactive Glossary

As you learn about each item, add notes, drawings, or sentences in the extra space. This will help you remember what the terms mean. Here is an example:

**fungi** (FUHN•jee) A group of organisms that get nutrients by decomposing other organisms

hongos Un grupo de organismos que obtienen sus nutrientes al descomponer otros organismos.

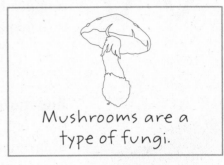

Mushrooms are a type of fungi.

## Glossary Pronunciation Key

With every glossary term, there is also a phonetic respelling. A phonetic respelling writes the word the way it sounds, which can help you pronounce new or unfamiliar words. Use this key to help you understand the respellings.

| Sound | As in | Phonetic Respelling | Sound | As In | Phonetic Respelling |
|-------|-------|---------------------|-------|-------|---------------------|
| a | bat | (BAT) | oh | over | (OH•ver) |
| ah | lock | (LAHK) | oo | pool | (POOL) |
| air | rare | (RAIR) | ow | out | (OWT) |
| ar | argue | (AR•gyoo) | oy | foil | (FOYL) |
| aw | law | (LAW) | s | cell | (SEL) |
| ay | face | (FAYS) | | sit | (SIT) |
| ch | chapel | (CHAP•uhl) | sh | sheep | (SHEEP) |
| e | test | (TEST) | th | that | (THAT) |
| | metric | (MEH•trik) | | thin | (THIN) |
| ee | eat | (EET) | u | pull | (PUL) |
| | feet | (FEET) | uh | medal | (MED•uhl) |
| | ski | (SKEE) | | talent | (TAL•uhnt) |
| er | paper | (PAY•per) | | pencil | (PEN•suhl) |
| | fern | (FERN) | | onion | (UHN•yuhn) |
| eye | idea | (eye•DEE•uh) | | playful | (PLAY•fuhl) |
| i | bit | (BIT) | | dull | (DUHL) |
| ing | going | (GOH•ing) | y | yes | (YES) |
| k | card | (KARD) | | ripe | (RYP) |
| | kite | (KYT) | z | bags | (BAGZ) |
| ngk | bank | (BANGK) | zh | treasure | (TREZH•er) |

# A

**amplitude** (AM•pluh•tood) A measure of the amount of energy in a wave. p. 156

**amplitud** Medida de la cantidad de energía en una onda.

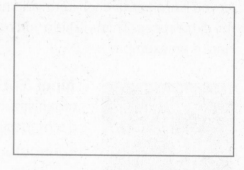

**aquatic fossil** (uh•KWAH•tik FAHS•uhl) The remains or traces of an organism that lived in water long ago. p. 492

**fósil acuático** Restos o vestigios de un organismo que vivió en el agua hace mucho tiempo.

# C

**collision** [kuh•LI•shuhn] The result of two objects bumping into each other. p. 128

**colisión** Resultado del choque entre dos objetos.

**constraint** (kuhn•STRAYNT) Something that limits what you are trying to do. p. 9

**restricción** Algo que limita lo que se está tratando de hacer.

**continent** (KON•tn•uhnt) One of the seven largest land areas on Earth. p. 409

**continente** Una de las siete áreas terrestres más grandes de la Tierra.

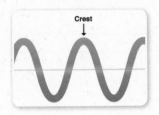

**crest** (KREST) The top part of a wave. p. 156

**cresta** Parte superior de una onda.

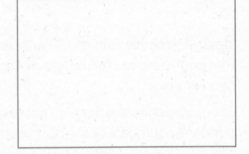

**criteria** (kry•TEER•ee•uh) The desirable features of a solution. p. 8

**criterios** Características deseables de una solución.

# D

**deposition** (dep•uh•ZISH•uhn) The dropping or settling of eroded materials. p. 359

**deposición** Caída o asentamiento de materiales erosionados.

# D

**desert** (DEZ•ert) An area of land that is very dry. p. 380

**desierto** Superficie de tierra muy seca.

**design process** (dih•ZYN PRAHS•es) A series of steps that engineers can follow to make solutions that meet a need or want.

**proceso de diseño** Serie de pasos que los ingenieros pueden seguir para desarrollar soluciones que cumplan con un requisito o una necesidad.

**drawback** (DRAW•bak) A disadvantage or problem. p. 538

**inconveniente** Desventaja o problema.

# E

**electric current** (ee•LEK•trik KER•uhnt) The flow of electric charges along a path. p. 72

**corriente eléctrica** Flujo de cargas eléctricas a lo largo de una trayectoria.

**elevation** (el•uh•VEY•shuhn)
The height of the land above sea level. p. 416

**elevación** Altura de la tierra sobre el nivel del mar.

**energy** (EN•er•jee) The ability to do work and cause changes in matter. p. 70

**energía** Capacidad de realizar una tarea y causar cambios en la materia.

**energy transfer** (EN•er•jee TRANZ•fuhr) The movement of energy from place to place or from one object to another. p. 78

**transferencia de energía** Movimiento de energía de un lugar a otro o de un objeto a otro.

**energy transformation** (EN•er•jee TRANZ•fuhr•may•shuhn) A change in energy from one form to another. p. 78

**transformación de la energía** Cambio en la energía, de una forma a otra.

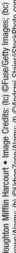

# E

**erosion** (uh•ROH•zhuhn) The process of moving sediment from one place to another. p. 359

**erosión** Proceso de mover el sedimento de un lugar a otro.

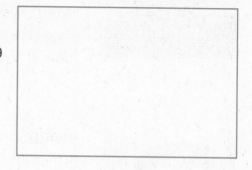

**external structures** (EX•tuhr•nuhl STRUK•churs) Those parts on the outside of a body or structure. p. 286

**estructuras externas** Partes que se encuentran fuera de un cuerpo o estructura.

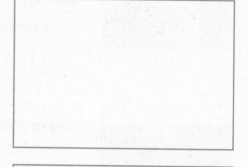

**extinct** (ex•STINGT) Describes a kind of thing that is no longer found on Earth. p. 484

**extinto** Describe cierto tipo de ser vivo que ya no se encuentra en la Tierra.

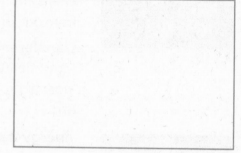

# F

**fertilization** (fur•tl• uh•ZEY• shuhn) The process when male and female reproductive parts join together. p. 257

**fertilización** Proceso en el que se unen los órganos reproductivos del macho y la hembra.

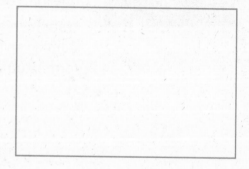

**fossil** (FAHS•uhl) The remains or traces of an organism that lived long ago. p. 484

**fósil** Restos o vestigios de un organismo que vivió hace tiempo.

# H

**heat** (HEET) The energy that moves between objects of different temperatures. p. 90

**calor** Energía que se mueve entre objetos con temperaturas distintas.

# I

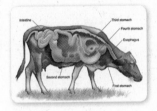

**internal structures** (IN•tuhr•nuhl STRUK•churs) Those parts on the inside of a body or structure. p. 306

**estructuras internas** Partes que se encuentran dentro de un cuerpo o estructura.

# L

**leaf** (LEEF) The part of a plant that makes food, using air, light, and water. p. 235

**hoja** Parte de la planta que es capaz de generar alimento usando aire, luz y agua.

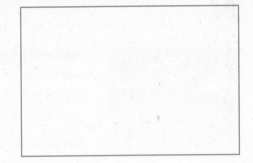

# N

**natural hazard** (NACH•er•uhl HAZ•urd) An earth process that threatens to harm people and property. p. 574

**peligro natural** Proceso terrestre que amenaza con dañar a personas y bienes.

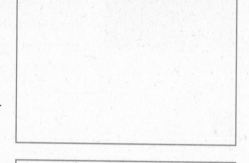

**natural resource** (NACH•er•uhl REE•sawrs) Materials found in nature that people and other living things use. p. 528

**recurso natural** Materiales que se encuentran en la naturaleza y que las personas y otros seres vivos utilizan.

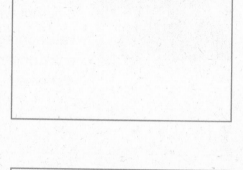

**nonrenewable resource** (nahn•rih•NOO•uh•buhl REE•sawrs) A resource that, once used, cannot be replaced in a reasonable amount of time. p. 529

**recurso no renovable** Recurso que, después de haber sido utilizado, no podrá ser reemplazado en un tiempo razonable.

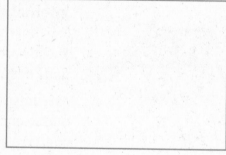

# O

**ocean trench** (OH•shuhn TRENCH) A deep valley in the ocean floor. p. 432

**fosa oceánica** Valle profundo en el suelo del océano.

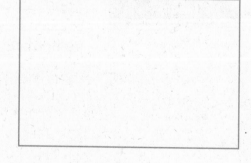

**opaque** (oh•PAYK) Not allowing light to pass through. p. 175

**opaco** Que no permite que la luz lo atraviese.

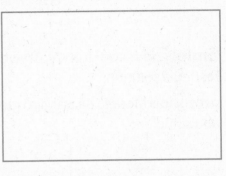

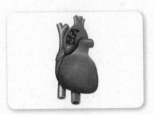

**organ** (AWR•guhn) A body part that is made of smaller parts that work together to do a certain job. p. 306

**órgano** Parte del cuerpo conformada por otras partes más pequeñas que trabajan juntas para cumplir una función determinada.

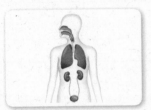

**organ system** (AWR•guhn SIS•tuhm) A group of organs that work together to do a job for the body. p. 306

**sistema de órganos** Grupo de órganos que trabaja en conjunto para realizar una tarea en el cuerpo.

# P

**pollination** (pol•uh•NAY•shuhn) The transfer of pollen in flowers or cones. p. 257

**polinización** Transferencia del polen en flores o conos.

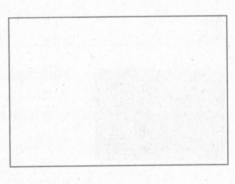

# P

**pollution** (puh•LOO•shuhn) Waste products that damage an ecosystem. p. 536

**contaminación** Todo desperdicio que daña un ecosistema.

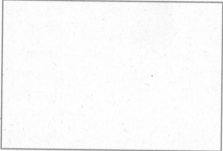

**prototype** (PROH•tuh•typ) A working model used for testing a solution.

**prototipo** Modelo de trabajo que se utiliza para probar una solución.

# R

**rain forest** (RAYN FOR•est) A dense forest found in regions with high heat and heavy rainfall. p. 380

**bosque lluvioso** Bosque denso que se encuentra en regiones de altas temperaturas y fuertes lluvias.

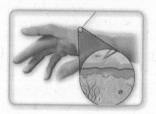

**receptors** (ree•SEP•turs) Special structures that send information about the environment from different parts of the body to the brain. p. 327

**receptores** Células nerviosas especiales que envían información acerca del ambiente desde la piel hasta el cerebro.

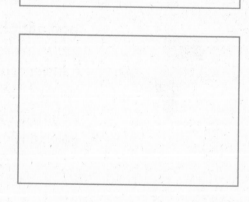

**reflection** (rih•FLEHK•shuhn)
The bouncing of light waves
when they encounter an
obstacle. p. 176

**reflejo** Rebote de las ondas
de luz cuando encuentran un
obstáculo.

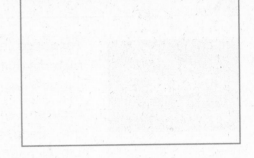

**relative age** (REL•uh•tiv AYJ)
The age of one thing compared
to another. p. 461

**edad relativa** Edad de una cosa
al compararla con otra.

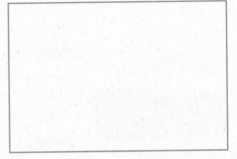

**renewable resource**
(rih•NOO•uh•buhl ree•SAWRS)
A resource that can be replaced
within a reasonable amount of
time. p. 550

**recurso renovable** Recurso
que puede ser reemplazado en
un tiempo razonable.

**reproduction**
(ree•pruh•DUHK•shuhn) To
have young, or more living
things of the same kind. p. 257

**reproducción** Tener cría o
generar más seres vivos del
mismo tipo.

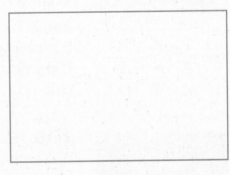

# R

**resource** (ree•SAWRS) Any material that can be used to satisfy a need. p. 528

**recurso** Cualquier material que pueda ser utilizado para satisfacer una necesidad.

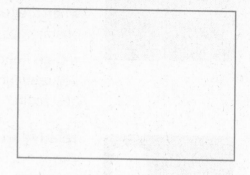

**root** (ROOT) A plant part that is usually underground and absorbs water and minerals from the soil. p. 235

**raíz** Parte de la planta que usualmente es subterránea y que absorbe agua y minerales del suelo.

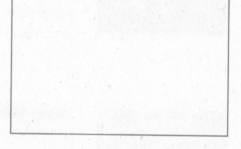

# S

**scale** (SKEYL) The part of a map that compares a distance on the map to a distance in the real world. p. 412

**escala** Parte de un mapa que compara la distancia en el mapa con la distancia en el mundo real.

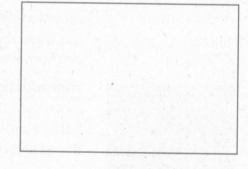

**seed** (SEED) The part of a plant that contains a new plant. p. 262

**semilla** Parte de la planta que contiene una nueva planta.

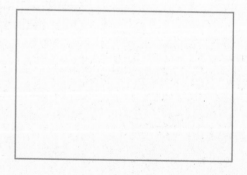

**spore** (SPOR) A reproductive structure of some plants, such as mosses and ferns, that can form a new plant. pp. 235, 263

**espora** Estructura reproductiva de algunas plantas, como los musgos y los helechos, que puede generar una nueva planta.

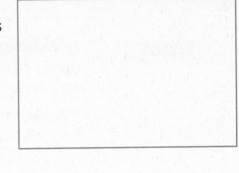

**stem** (STEM) The part of a plant that holds it up and has tubes that carry water, minerals, and nutrients through the plant. p. 235

**tallo** Parte de la planta que la sostiene y que tiene conductos que llevan agua, minerales y nutrientes a través de toda la planta.

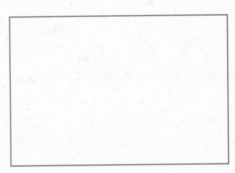

# T

**terrestrial fossil** (tuh•RES•tree•uhl FAHS•uhl) The remains or traces of an organism that lived on land long ago. p. 492

**fósil terrestre** Restos o vestigios de un organismo que vivió en la tierra hace mucho tiempo.

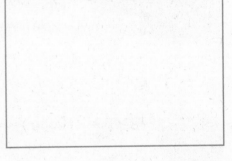

**translucent** (trahns•LOO•suhnt) Letting some light through. p. 175

**translúcido** Que deja pasar parte de la luz.

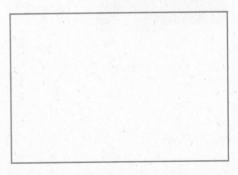

# T

### transparent
(trahns•PAIR•uhnt) Letting all light through. p. 175

**transparente** Que deja pasar toda la luz.

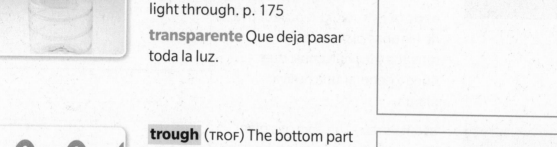

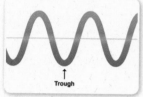

### trough (TROF) The bottom part of a wave. p. 156

**depresión** Parte inferior de una onda.

# V

### vibrate (VY•brayt) To move back and forth. p. 102

**vibrar** Moverse hacia delante y hacia atrás.

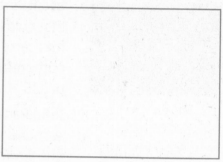

### volume (VAHL•yoom) How loud or soft a sound is. p. 158

**volumen** Cuán alto o bajo es un sonido.

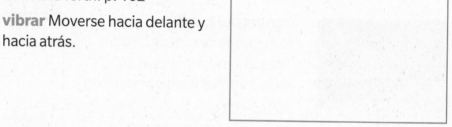

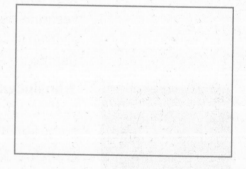

**wave** (WAYV) The up-and-down movement of surface water. It can also be a disturbance that carries energy through space. p. 149

**ola** Movimiento hacia arriba y hacia abajo de la superficie del agua.

**onda** Alteración que lleva energía por el espacio.

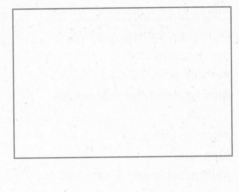

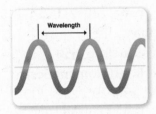

**wavelength** (WAYV•length) The distance between a point on one wave and the identical point on the next wave. p. 156

**longitud de onda** Distancia entre un punto en una onda y ese mismo punto en la próxima onda.

**weathering** (WETH•er•ing) The breaking down of rocks on Earth's surface into smaller pieces. p. 359

**desgaste** Descomposición de las piedras de la superficie terrestre en piezas más pequeñas.

# Index

## A

acoustic engineers, 38–39
aerial photo, 406
air pollution, 73, 540–542
Akaroa Head (New Zealand), 459
algae farming, 73
Alps, 459
Alvarez, Luis and Walter, 514
amber, 493
amplitude, 156–158, 162–163
Anderson, Clayton, 249
anechoic chamber, 34, 36–37
animals
    adaptations to environment, 381
    alpaca, 290
    ammonite, 492, 495
    antelope, 289
    ants, 287, 493
    archerfish, 186
    Bactrian camel, 381
    bat, 287, 338, 339
    beaver, 384
    birds, 290, 309, 317
    body coverings, 286, 290–292, 296–298
    cat, 336
    circulatory system, 306, 308–310
    clam, 493
    corals, 493, 495
    cow, 317
    crocodile, 309
    crustaceans, 505
    digestive system, 314–318
    dog, 336
    dolphin, 287, 325
    dragonfly, 493
    eagle, 289
    elephant, 219–220, 333
    fish, 186, 309, 492, 495–496, 505
    frog, 287, 289
    gecko, 285, 294
    greater wax moth, 339
    Irish elk, 488
    jellyfish, 317
    lizards, 285, 294
    meerkat, 382
    mosasaur, 489
    mosquito, 289
    mountain lion, 289
    mouse, 333
    mouth parts, 289, 293
    peacock mantis shrimp, 324, 339
    pigeon, 287, 336
    plesiosaur, 484
    polyp, 495
    respiratory system, 306–309
    sambar deer, 381
    sandfish, 294
    sea cucumber, 290
    shark, 287, 317
    snail, 492
    snakes, 152, 290, 336, 505
    sounds of, 155, 219–220
    structures for movement, 287–288, 293, 295
    termite, 384
    tubeworm, 289
    turtles and tortoises, 290, 501
anther, 256
anvil (ear), 337
aquadynamic testing, 35
arch, rock, 475
argument, 50, 267, 291, 298
artery, 306, 310
Artiles, Mayra, 83

## B

Badlands of South Dakota, 464–465
bark (tree), 235, 237
base isolator, 581
batteries, 74, 78–79, 82–83, 567–568
beach erosion, 151, 358, 369, 396
beak, 293
beats (tuning), 164
binary code, 210–211, 214–215
binoculars, 189
biomass fuel, 73, 550
biomimicry (biomimetics), 292, 294–295, 299–300
Birling Gap, England, 358
bits (in binary code), 210, 212–213
bladder, 316
Block, Adrienne, 442
blood, 306–310
brain, 190–191, 326, 337
brainstorm, 601
breathing, 306–307, 308, 311–313
bridge (rock formation), 475
British Thermal Unit (Btu), 532
Buckley Formation (Antarctica), 459
buffering, electronic, 212–213
buoy, 150–151, 606
burr, 292
burrow, 382

## C

cable, telegraph, 204–205
camera lens, 188
canyon formation, 462, 471–472, 475
carbon dioxide, 90, 316

© Houghton Mifflin Harcourt

Earth's history from, 458–459, 462

fossils in, 464

inferring environments in, 465, 506–507

interpreting, 458, 464, 512

modeling, 458, 468–470

pressure and heat in, 458, 474

relative age of, 460, 462–463, 506–507

weathering and erosion of, 459, 471–472, 475, 511

**rocks.** *See also* **rock layers**

formation of, 460

in freezing and thawing, 362–363, 396

in glaciers, 364–365, 475

plant roots and, 382

pressure and heat and, 474

sedimentary, 463

weathering and erosion of, 151, 459, 471–472, 475, 511

**role playing,** 601

**root hairs,** 383

**roots,** 234–236, 238, 240, 247, 382, 385

**ROV (Remotely Operated Vehicle),** 433

**Ruiz,** Vanessa, 319

## S

**safety**

disaster supply kit, 581

family emergency plan, 607

fire extinguishers, 591

laboratory, XVIII

thermal imaging devices, 94

**sandbag,** 597, 606

**sandblasting,** 386

**sand dune,** 390, 396

**sand fence,** 399–400

**sand transport,** 388–391

**satellites**

in flood prediction, 610

in hurricane detection, 606

maps from, 407

photographs from, 407, 606

signals from, 153, 200, 212, 217

in wildfire detection, 584

**scale (maps),** 408, 412–413

**schools of fish,** 492

**science,** 55–56, 544

**scytale,** 207

**secret codes,** 206–207

**sediment,** 355–356, 359, 364, 388

**sedimentary rocks,** 463

**seeds,** 237, 258, 262, 265–267, 268–270, 292

**seeing,** 324, 336, 339

**seismograph,** 473

**seismometer,** 473, 574–575, 582, 584–585

**self-pollination,** 259

**semi circular canal (ear),** 337

**senses**

echolocation, 325, 338

extreme, 339

nervous system, 326–329

reflexes, 329

sight, 324, 336, 339

smell, 333

taste, 334–335

**sepal,** 256

**shear core,** 581

**shear wall,** 581

**skeletal system,** 326

**skin,** 286, 290–291, 316, 327–328

**slithering,** 152

**small intestine,** 314

**smart roads,** 372

**smell receptor,** 333

**smoke signal,** 203

**solar energy**

solar cells, 79, 561

solar cooker, 99–101, 561

solar hot water heater, 562–566

solar panels, 95, 176, 549, 552, 554, 561

solar rays, 96

**solution (to problem)**

in *Can You Solve It?*, for example, 5, 19, 23, 41, 45

in *Hands-On Activity*, for example, 9, 31, 46, 99

in lessons, for example, 17, 24–25, 38, 49–51, 217

**SONAR technology,** 433

**sound energy,** 78, 88, 103–107, 154

**sound waves**

amplitude of, 156–158, 162–163

in anechoic chambers, 34, 36–37

canceled, 163

in cell phones, 216–217

direction of motion in, 154–155

Doppler effect, 165

from elephant stomps, 219–220

hearing, 18, 337–338

infrasounds, 219

in matter, 155

measuring, 40

in SONAR technology, 433

from vibrations, 102–103

wavelength of, 159

**space exploration**

astronauts, 249

energy transfer on Mars, 131–132

International Space Station, 170, 249

waves in, 153, 155

**speakers,** 103

**speed and energy,** 118–119, 128–129

**spinal cord,** 326, 329

**spines (animal),** 290

**spines (plant),** 235, 237

© Houghton Mifflin Harcourt

© Houghton Mifflin Harcourt